PaddleMore in Lo
and the Trossachs

A GUIDE FOR CANOES, KAYAKS AND SUPS

By Grant Dolier and Tom Kilpatrick

First published 2021
Published in Great Britain 2021 by Pesda Press
Tan y Coed Canol
Ceunant
Caernarfon,
Gwynedd,
LL55 4RN

Copyright © 2021 PaddleMore

ISBN: 978-1-906095-76-5

Contains Ordnance Survey data © Crown copyright and database right 2021
Maps by Bute Cartographic

Printed in Poland, www.lfbooksevices.co.uk

Acknowledgements

This book wouldn't have been possible without the input and influence of so many other people and we would like to extend our gratitude to them in this section.

First and foremost, we would like to extend our thanks to Franco and all the team at Pesda Press. When we approached them with what we thought was the outline of a book and a great idea, we had no idea how far we still had to go to reach the finished product. Their help and guidance through the process has been invaluable.

The undying support of our partners, Ellie and Beth, has spurred us both on when things seemed to be hitting dead ends. Not only that, but they willingly come on trips with us, and have put up with us and been nothing but positive about our paddling partnership for years; without them we would never have written this book.

Speaking of our bromance, we couldn't go through a whole acknowledgments section without some recognition of the place we first met. Back in 2013, Moose moved to Scotland to work at the Lochgoilhead Centre, coincidentally the same year Grant moved back to the centre having worked abroad. Within weeks we were paddling together and the friendship flourished. Without Neil Baird offering us both jobs, a decision we're certain he wondered about for years afterwards, we might never have got on the river together.

Finally, we would like to thank everyone we've ever paddled with. From the first people to take us out on the water as much younger versions of who we are today, to those we guide with, or who have run courses for us, or who have simply been there to go paddling with.

There really is nothing half so worth doing than simply messing about in boats, and we're always grateful when other people want to join us.

Important Notice – Disclaimer

Canoeing, kayaking and paddleboarding are healthy outdoor activities that carry some degree of risk. They involve adventurous travel, often away from close habitation. Guidebooks give an idea of where to access a river, where to egress, the level of difficulty and the nature of the hazards to be encountered.

However, nature being what it is, river valleys are changed by time and erosion, water levels vary considerably with rain, and man-made features can be updated or altered – therefore weirs, walls and landings are not always as expected. Coastal sections, large lakes and estuaries are also subject to change due to wind and weather. This guidebook is no substitute for personal inspection at the time of paddling, and your own risk assessment and judgement. Your decision to paddle or not, and any consequences arising from that decision, is your responsibility.

Contents

⌖ Local Adventure \ Photo PaddleMore

Welcome to Loch Lomond & The Trossachs National Park

Good choice.

Loch Lomond & The Trossachs National Park is long established as a playground for paddlers and attracts visitors from all over the world. Loch Lomond itself has over eighty kilometres of shoreline to explore, but there is so much more to the park. The twenty-two navigable lochs range from the vast sea lochs around Loch Long to small inland bodies such as Loch Chon. The rivers vary from relaxed meandering waterways like the Balvaig to the steep white water of the River Falloch and everything in between.

This vast array of options in such close proximity makes this park the perfect place for every paddler of any level, looking for whatever type of adventure. The area is also outstandingly beautiful and it is commonplace to see deer and red squirrels playing on the shores, as well as the many other species of mammal, bird and water life which call this park home.

So why have we written this book?

Our ethos is simple; more people, more paddling, more often.

Rather than limiting you to one discipline, we have focused on all options within the national park. Whether you want hardcore white water, multi-day touring trips or a relaxing afternoon exploring sheltered water with your family, you'll find all that and much more in this book.

This 'much more' element includes those make or break aspects of many trips; where to get a good coffee, bacon roll, or somewhere to stay with a hot fire and a cold drink. We have also tried to include relevant, interesting information, stories, and tips from our many years of exploring the park.

You may be wondering what gives us the authority to write about the National Park. Understandably. Collectively we have over twenty-five years of professional guiding experience in the park as well as countless personal trips on the rivers and lochs. Driven by our love of exploration and enduring bromance, and much to the dismay of our partners, we continue to spend days off paddling new areas and coming up with wild adventures.

What is PaddleMore

We're just a couple of paddlers, passionate about promoting paddling. It doesn't matter if it's your family's first time afloat on a paddleboard, or you're a beardy multi-day canoe tripper, or you're hucking 20 metre drops with the crew – we're with you!

Meet the team!

GRANT DOLIER

Grant started paddling over fifteen years ago on the west coast of Scotland. Since then he has explored more of Scotland than most people could imagine. His experiences in the UK and working overseas in the Ardèche, coupled with his extensive knowledge of paddlesports, make him a highly sought-after coach and guide. He is backed by Hōu Canoes, is involved with Scottish Canoe Association as part of the Environmental and Access Team, and supports Scouts Scotland with paddlesports provision across Scotland.

© Meet the team, Grant and Tom \ Photo PaddleMore

TOM 'MOOSE' KILPATRICK

Moose started his paddling life on the ponds and rivers in the south-east of England. He has slowly worked his way north and has spent the last few years working his way through all things Scottish. As well as being a very experienced and knowledgeable coach and guide across Scotland and the rest of the UK, he spent a summer in Norway and a month in Nepal; apparently they weren't bad.

THE TEAM

We started paddling together in 2013, when Moose finally saw the light and moved to Scotland. The bromance flourished and, to the dismay of our partners, most of our days off were spent together.

Together we have paddled and swam on countless lochs and rivers in Scotland. We have guided trips together, explored new regions and shared our favourite paddling spots with anyone who will come with us. Abroad, we have paddled on the Soča together as part of a European adventure and the Noguera Pallaresa after an epic journey from Aviemore to Spain.

If it floats, we love to paddle it!

Safety First

Danger never takes a day off!

Paddlesports is an inherently risky sport. This book is designed as a guide to the area, written by paddlers who want to share their love of the sport. With that in mind, while we have tried to consider all sorts of weather, river levels and paddler abilities, we cannot encompass everything.

We want to encourage as many paddlers as possible in all sorts of places, but it is important to be aware of your personal abilities and those of your group. Even the most tame-looking waterway can become wild in the wrong conditions and rivers can swell quickly. Make sure you have the right training and understanding relevant to the environment you want to paddle in.

Injuries and accidents may occur while taking part in paddlesports. Prepare yourself with safety equipment and knowledge. Emergency and rescue services are always on hand, but only if you have means to contact them and know where you are. It's also worthwhile telling someone you're going on the water; remember to let them know when you're off so they know you're safe.

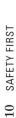

River grading

Ungraded   Ungraded sections of slow moving rivers where the group could paddle upstream against the flow (not involving the shooting of, or playing on, weirs or running rapids).

Grade 1   Moving water with occasional small rapids.
                    Few or no obstacles to negotiate.

Grade 2   Small rapids featuring regular waves. Some manoeuvring required.

Grade 2 (3)   The overall standard of the run is grade 2, but there may be a few (normally one or two) grade 3 rapids that can be portaged if required.

Grade 3   Most rapids will have irregular waves and hazards that need avoiding. More difficult manoeuvring will be required but routes are normally obvious. Scouting from shore is occasionally necessary to maintain line of sight.

Grade 4   Large rapids that require careful manoeuvring. Scouting from the shore is often necessary and rescue is usually difficult. Kayakers should be able to roll before tackling these rapids. In the event of a mishap, there is significant risk of loss, damage and / or injury.

Grade 4(5)   The overall standard of the run is grade 4, but there may be a few (normally one or two) grade 5 rapids that can be portaged if required.

Grade 5   Extremely difficult – long and very violent rapids with severe hazards. Continuous, powerful, confused water makes route finding difficult and scouting from the shore is essential. Precise manoeuvring is critical and for kayakers, rolling ability needs to be 100%. Rescue is very difficult or impossible and in the event of a mishap there is significant hazard to life.

Source – *British Canoeing Environmental Definitions and Deployment Guidance for Instructors, Coaches and Leaders*

Navigating this Guide

We have split the national park into four different regions: Loch Lomond, The Trossachs, Breadalbane, and Cowal

Within these regions we have described the lochs, with Loch Lomond itself being divided into three distinct sections, followed by the rivers which link them. The final section outlines six long distance routes. These are multi-day trips, which often combine several of these regions.

For each route the following Quick Reference information is provided if apropriate:

Get on/off	Access Grid Reference / Egress Grid Reference. These will be the main points outlined in the route, but other options may be given further down in the text.
Time required	This is a rough approximation based on our experiences, but will vary depending on a number of factors including your ability, your chosen craft and the weather conditions.
Distance	Distance in kilometres of the prescribed route.
Parking/shuttle	Access parking / shuttle parking. The access parking is often limited and we have suggested other options in the Trip Overview where this is the case. The shuttle parking is for the egress.
Optimum water levels	Only relevant to rivers, these mainly relate to SEPA (Scottish Environmental Protection Agency) levels which can be found on their website.
River grade	The grade of the river at usual paddling levels (only relevant to rivers). This may vary with water levels and it is incumbent on you to read the river as you paddle it. As we all know, grading is somewhat variable and situation dependent. This is only a guidebook, the decision to paddle a rapid or not is up to you on the day.

Map symbols in this book

△	start		🏋	portage
◎	finish		- - → - - →	described route
△	alternative start		X	campsite
◎	alternative finish		• Placename	town / buildings
			▲ name Peakname	significant peak
			🏰	castle

Equipment

The kit you take on a paddling trip depends on many things: where you plan to go, weather conditions, who you're accompanied by, and many more.

Regardless, there are certain things which should be with you, or at least among the group, on each trip:

- **The right craft for the environment** – This should be kitted out with proper buoyancy and safety features. This is explored more deeply in the next section. Make sure you take a paddle!

- **Personal flotation** – This should be checked frequently and used within manufacturer recommendations.

- **Helmets** – These are recommended for river environments but it is at the discretion of the wearer (or non-wearer). We strongly recommend the wearing of them for all white water and shallow rivers.

- **Appropriate clothing** – For the environment, weather and craft. Pick your clothes to suit, and remember there's always a possibility that you might get wet.

- **Spare warm clothing** – Scottish weather changes fast and it's not uncommon to experience all four seasons in one day. Spare layers can also be used to keep casualties warm.

- **First aid kit** – You should make sure you know how to use this and have been appropriately trained in what to do in a water-borne situation.

- **Emergency group shelter** – Somewhere to stay warm if you get into difficulties, either a tent, tarp or bothy bag for the whole group. Along with warm clothing, this not only keeps the casualty warm but can prevent the rest of the group becoming casualties themselves.

- **Means of communication** – There is often patchy phone signal in the National Park so other means of communication (VHF radios, GPS trackers, flares) can be useful. Make sure you know how to use these as misuse can land you in trouble.

- **Specialist WW rescue equipment** – Make sure you have the knowledge to use this kit and that it is suited to the environment. There's no use carrying bags of ropes and chains of karabiners if you don't know how to use them.

Top tip: Streamline your safety kit. Everything should serve a purpose but make sure you've accounted for all reasonable situations.

Choosing your craft

If it floats, you can probably paddle it. This doesn't necessarily mean you should.

Paddling the wrong craft is like wearing the wrong shoes. The right boat type will make your journey safer, easier and much more enjoyable. Length, width and height of a boat all make a difference, as do attachment points and kit-stowing arrangements. We have not prescribed a particular craft, but have given information to allow you to make an informed decision.

In this section we will detail a range of boats. It is not an exhaustive list but it includes the more popular and well-used craft. We have avoided recommending any one particular craft but have hopefully given you some options and things to consider.

STAND UP PADDLEBOARDS (SUP)

Contrary to popular belief you don't have to stand up to use one of these. They are becoming increasingly popular and ranges of SUPs are diversifying. There are boards designed for white water, touring trips or recreational. Inflatable SUPs are popular with people who have to travel, their deflated size suiting hold luggage on a plane or the boot of a rental car.

These should be used with leashes and fully inflated to recommended pressure before entering the water.

CANOE

A traditional approach to taking to the water, the use of canoes dates back thousands of years. These are multi-purpose boats but do differ in design and usage. Depending on whether you want to paddle the boat solo or with a family, expedition over lochs or paddle rivers, your boat choice may change.

Canoes usually require buoyancy bags or blocks at either end and have several attachment points for ropes or painters – for securing, attaching or rescuing boats. Canoes differ from kayaks because they are paddled with a single blade, but can be open top or closed cockpits. Generally when we refer to canoes we mean the traditional open-topped style.

WHITE-WATER KAYAK

Usually closed cockpit, these are shorter boats generally 9' (2.75m) or less. This shorter length allows greater manoeuvrability in rivers, ideal for quick moves in white water. Air bags, foam pillars and attachment points on the outside of the boat are all safety features on these boats, strengthening and allowing easier rescues. Within white-water kayaks, boat design differs between long creek boats and short playboats and it's worth doing some research as to what type of boat would suit your needs.

TOURING / SEA KAYAK

Touring kayaks and sea kayaks are longer than white-water boats. Usually 13' (4m)+ these are narrower with a V-shaped hull which allows these boats to glide gently through the water. Their length and speed allows them to cover much longer distances than their white-water counterparts.

These boats tend to have bulkheads to stop water flooding the entire boat in the event of a swim. Additionally they have hatches for gear storage and roped lines around them, as well as bungee cord, for attachment points and spare paddles.

CROSSOVER KAYAKS

As the name suggests, these kayaks blur the lines between our touring / sea and white-water kayaks. They often have hatches and bulkheads similar to touring / sea boats, but are shorter and more manoeuvrable, like white-water boats. Although they have many of the great features from the two types of boats, they also have limitations in each discipline. These can be a great option for mixed environment trips.

SIT ON TOP KAYAKS

Open-top kayaks act as a stable platform and are often the most appropriate craft for beginners or younger paddlers. They are easy to climb back onto if you fall off, and great for shorter journeys on open water. There are sit on top kayaks designed for touring as well as white water, therefore in these cases can be considered in those categories.

OTHER INFLATABLES

We haven't forgotten about rafts, inflatable kayaks or swimming-pool toys. These are all great ways to get out on the water, but as they're not what we use regularly we decided to leave these up to your discretion. As long as you're out safely enjoying the water, we don't mind how you do it.

Planning your trip \ Photo PaddleMore

Planning

Even the most experienced paddlers plan their trips. Sometimes it's simply a matter of checking river levels, wind conditions or what time the sun sets. Other times you might plan for days, painstakingly checking and rechecking mapped routes, weather forecasts, campsites and lists of kit.

Planning and pre-trip organisation takes many different forms, but is vital to success. On longer trips it's worth establishing where you can cut short if you are forced by the weather. Sometimes we're forced to change or abandon plans completely. This book will offer you alternatives which may be more suitable in challenging conditions.

The trip should be appropriate for everyone in the group. As always you are only as strong as your weakest member; this is not always the same as the least experienced. People paddle at different levels and might have different aims for the trip. Be sure it suits everyone and isn't taking them into environments well above their skill level.

Expeditioning

Perhaps one of the best ways to experience The Loch Lomond & The Trossachs National Park is to spend a night under the stars. There are incredible places to camp in the park, many of which can only be accessed via the water, including around one hundred islands.

Expeditioning brings with it a whole new element of planning and organisation and many other authors delve deeper into these subjects. In short, be sure to have (as well as the kit we have mentioned) appropriate sleeping shelter, sleeping bag, sleeping mat, stove and food. It's also useful to have some means to purify water to make it safe to drink.

© Packing for a trip | Photo PaddleMore

PICKING YOUR CAMPSITE

Extra consideration should be given to everything discussed previously in the planning section. Campsites should be chosen to suit these considerations too. Many island campsites have flooded because of fast-rising rivers; campers become shore-bound when Scotland has shown its wild side, unexpectedly and the loch turned wild and rough.

Scotland has some of the most dramatic and incredible wild spaces in the UK (and arguably the world). Pragmatic access laws allow us to play freely, but responsibly, in these environments. The National Park was unfortunately seeing a steady increase in anti-social behaviour and irresponsible camping, and brought seasonal by-laws into practice in 2017. Camping in certain areas of the park now requires permits between 01 March and 30 September.

Don't panic though. Wild camping is still absolutely fine throughout a great deal of the park. The management zones are predominantly roadside and in the more populated areas. For a more comprehensive explanation visit: http://www.lochlomond-trossachs.org/things-to-do/camping/. You can find information on the by-law, wild camping and how to get a permit if you need one. There is also information on what to do if you need a poo.

Leave No Trace

If you're the sort of person who wants to explore the Loch Lomond & The Trossachs National Park, we can safely assume you're the sort of person who already knows about Leave No Trace. We all enjoy being out without the blight of litter or human waste on the river bank to put your boat in.

Leave No Trace goes deeper than this and should be at the forefront of all our trips out. To show how serious it is, we got someone else to write this bit. Neil Baird swans around an outdoor activity centre calling himself the manager but is only really responsible for emptying the bins within the park. Joking aside, he is a Leave No Trace Trainer, providing training courses to other outdoor professionals.

Leave No Trace – by Neil Baird

How do you share information about a beautiful place and then protect that place from being spoiled due to excessive visitors?

This question is the question a national park authority must wrestle with daily but is also the origins of an organisation called Leave No Trace. Leave No Trace was set up in America to help protect the national parks through education and training after dealing with large numbers of people using the areas irresponsibly.

📷 *Neil Baird*

Some people may have heard of Leave No Trace or be aware of Leave No Trace principles but what does this really mean?

The aim is not to make everyone become an eco-warrior but to let people start making informed decisions around their own personal ethics about how they use the outdoors. Attending a Leave No Trace course will not solve every issue associated with the outdoors or instantly solve problems but it will gradually make you question what you do and why you take the course of action you do.

Leave No Trace identified seven of the most common problems in the outdoors and developed seven principles that created a framework to educate participants in methods to mitigate these recurring problem areas. I will give a quick summary of the seven principles and identify a simple step for each that will help you protect the environment you operate within. More ideas and principles can be learned through attending a one-day introduction to Leave No Trace where tutors can discuss your specific environments and activities to give ideas and principles that will help each individual.

PLAN AHEAD AND PREPARE

Planning ahead can allow you to gain more from your outdoor experience. Think about where you are going and what you plan to do while questioning your impact. Try to avoid honey pots or areas that you know will be busy or crowded and think about the time you are going. If you go earlier or later will you gain more from being there during quite times?

BE CONSIDERATE OF OTHERS

Not everyone will have the training, knowledge or education within the outdoors that you have. Be patient with everyone and try to help others make ethical decisions. If you are able to help others make small steps towards positive use of the outdoors every gain will help the environment. Conflict in the outdoors between users will help no one and detract from the very experience and reason you are there.

RESPECT FARM ANIMALS AND WILDLIFE

The nature of visiting the outdoors means we will be entering an environment that is the habitat of wildlife and farm animals. Our very presence can have an impact on animals yet we can take some simple steps to minimise our impact. Respectfully observe animals and wildlife from a distance and be willing to move away if you observe changes in behaviour caused by your presence. Be aware of nesting and mating seasons and avoid disturbing these activities. Keep an eye out for signs informing you of restrictions or requesting you to change your route due to wildlife. Those travelling with dogs should be particularly aware of other animals and keep dogs under control. Livestock and wild animals can be unpredictable if they feel threatened by people or dogs. And you could inadvertently place yourself at risk.

TRAVEL AND CAMP ON DURABLE GROUND

Every time we move through an environment, we will have an impact, mostly small, but sometimes we can have more impact on the ground than others. Try to stay on trails and be willing to get your feet dirty rather than moving to the side of muddy sections expanding the trail wider. Be aware of sensitive areas such as sand dunes or bogs and try where possible to avoid crossing areas that are sensitive or have special vegetation or characteristics that make it of interest.

LEAVE WHAT YOU FIND

We visit the outdoors for many reasons but mostly the beauty and attractiveness of the area is from the things within it whether this is plants, rocks, vegetation or historic items.

If we remove these items to take them with us, we will remove the very reason we have visited the area in the first place. Take time to enjoy things in their setting and leave them there for others to enjoy. Be aware that some plants, animals and historic sites may be protected and removing items could get you into trouble without realising your mistakes.

DISPOSE OF WASTE PROPERLY

Anyone using the outdoors for recreation has an obligation to tidy that area before leaving. Try to reduce the waste we produce by planning ahead but be prepared to take any rubbish with us. Know how to deal with human waste and dispose of our own waste in a way that will not affect animals, watercourses or other users of the area. Have a plan on how you will deal with all of your waste and ensure it is disposed of ethically.

MINIMISE THE EFFECTS OF FIRE

Fire can be one of the most devastating elements of nature. We must implement techniques which limit the effects of fire on the environment, but implement them ethically. Use fire circles that are already there; do not make new fire circles. Have fires on beaches below the tide line or use mound and pan fires to limit impact. If you must have a fire think about the size of your fire and keep it small and manageable.

The seven principles make up the Leave No Trace principles and despite giving a quick overview of some of the techniques and steps that can be taken to limit your impact, nothing will replace completing a full Leave No Trace course for yourself or organisations that will help shape your own ethics and morals in the outdoors.

Evening paddle \ Photo PaddleMore

Loch Lomond

Arguably Scotland's best known body of water, Loch Lomond (Loch Laomainn) offers an enormous seventy square kilometres of water to paddle on, as well as twenty-two islands and many more islets to explore. These islands have rich and varied history and at one time or another most of them have been inhabited. There are castles, priories, wallabies (yes wallabies!), and wild stories which bring them alive. Vikings raided any number of these islands, when they portaged their boats from Loch Long in the west at Tarbet, before leaving down the River Leven.

Geographically, Loch Lomond is something of an entrance to the highlands. The chain of islands, which stretch across from Connich Hill on the east to Cruach Dhubh on the west, sit directly on the highland fault boundary. Standing along this line you can see a clear distinction between the hills to the south and the rugged, highland mountains to the north.

The tourism here may mean that sections of the loch feel busier than other areas of the park, but it is easy enough to escape the crowds once you're on the water. There are countless shops and cafés all round the loch, and you'll have no shortage of options for stocking up or grabbing a coffee on the way.

Loch Lomond itself is so big that we have divided it up into three distinct trips, but these can be combined to create an excellent multi-day trip where you'll be treated to some of the most magnificent sunsets and landscapes that Scotland has to offer.

OPEN WATER

1 The Beautiful South

2 Island Explore

3 Northern Circuit

RIVERS

4 Endrick Water

5 River Falloch – WW Grade 4/5

6 Luss Water – WW Grade: 3/4(5)

7 River Leven

📷 *Heading to Inchcailloch \ Photo PaddleMore*

© Padding south past Clairinsh \ Photo PaddleMore

1 The Beautiful South

Get on / off	NS 411 922 / NS 386 823
Time required	3+ hours
Distance	16km
Parking / shuttle:	NS 411 922 / NS 386 822

Introduction

The busiest area of the park, Lomond Shores at Balloch, is a popular day out for the locals in Glasgow. If you can tear yourself away from the shops, cafés and the sea-life centre here, the Loch Lomond Distillery is also in town and worth a visit, so long as you're not driving the shuttle. Balloch itself has a number of supermarkets and shops at which to stock up before heading out for the day.

Just north of Balloch, you will often see seaplanes landing and taking off from Arden. These come and go regularly and are worth looking out for, they're great to watch – as long as they're moving away from you.

There are a number of islands along the way. Inchcailloch, or the Island of the Old Woman, so named after the ancient convent on the island, is accessible from Balmaha

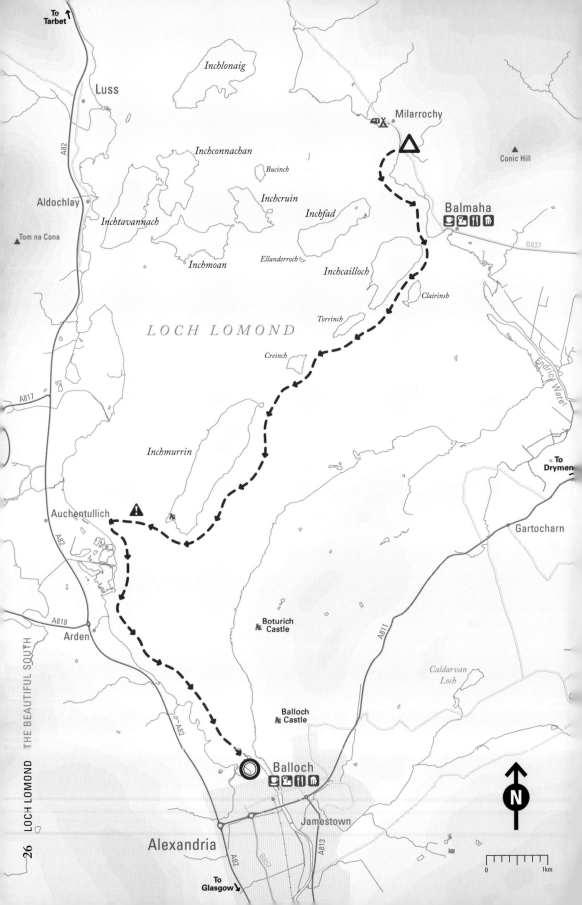

via a regular ferry. This island is adorned with bluebells and is a popular trip for families during the summer. Inchmurrin, however, has an altogether more unusual past. The Earl of Lennox's castle on the island was commonly used by nobility as a refuge, due to its remote location. In later years this island was also used as mental asylum, and where they also sent unmarried women to give birth.

Haggis hurling

In 1984 the island was the location for a world record haggis hurl by Alan Pettigrew, a record which lasted until 2011. Rob Dunseath was responsible for the rebirth of this 'ancient' sport, after he placed an advert in a local paper advertising the "World Haggis Hurling Championships" at the Gathering of the Clans in 1977. He later came clean about the hoax, claiming he and his friends wrote it as a joke. The sport continues despite this and competitions take place as far away as Australia and America.

Trip overview

Milarrochy has a large car park, toilets and showers and is on the course of the west highland way, so sees its fair share of visitors.

This route can be paddled either direction between Balloch and Milarrochy, or as a 'there and back' route if you have the energy. If you lunch in Balloch you have no end to the options available to you but it may be busy with other paddlers in Drumkinnon Bay. If you choose to start from Balloch and paddle this route out to Balmaha, the Oak Tree pub in town is a great choice for lunch. Here you can also see the statue of Tom Weir, most famous for Weir's Way, a TV show in the 70s and 80s where he explored Scotland's history and people as he walked his way around the country.

This trip is usually relatively sheltered, but the crossing from Inchmurrin to Auchentullich is just over a kilometre and wind can funnel through here. In these conditions we recommend crossing between Inchmurrin and Knockour instead. The crossings between Inchmurrin, Creinch and Torrinch can also become challenging in windier conditions. If it's looking as if the wind may build, perhaps consider the Island Explore route instead, where you will generally have more shelter around the island chain.

The route

Head out from Milarrochy and then south-west toward Balmaha, the starting point for the walk up Conich Hill.

From here make the short crossing to Inchcailloch. We usually head round the north side of this island as it allows you spectacular views up the loch. If there is a northerly

wind blowing however, go south around to make use of the island to shelter yourself. On the western shores of the island there is a campsite and composting toilets, perfect if you want to book in and make this an overnight trip.

Head out from here to Torrinch, or feel free to visit Clairinsh if time allows. From Torrinch cross to Creinch. Wind can channel through here and make it difficult crossing, the same applies from here to Inchmurrin. The fetch can build if the wind is coming from the north, and this should be carefully considered before undertaking the crossing.

Depending on the wind conditions, there are two options from here. From the south-west of Inchmurrin, either head east to the jetty at Auchentullich, or south-east to Knockour.

From either of these, head in a southerly direction along the shore towards Balloch where the trip either ends, or where you turn around and head back.

Maid of the Loch

Why not visit the *Maid of the Loch*? The last paddle steamer built in Britain, she allowed tourists to explore the water for 29 years until 1981. She now sits at Balloch pier and is open to the public throughout the summer.

© Loch Lomond Island chain \ Photo PaddleMore

2 Island Explore

Get on / off	NS 360 932
Time required	3+ hours
Distance	14km
Parking / shuttle	NS 359 931

Introduction

The island chain on Loch Lomond marks the geographical start of the highlands. From Conic Hill behind Balmaha to Cruach Dubh on the west, across eight distinct islands. This trip is a historian's dream, each island bringing with it some form of Scottish history or heritage adding to the underlying geological importance of the place. Not only that, but it is one of the most stunning paddling trips in Scotland. The views to the south are of rolling hills, while the striking mountains of the north puncture the skyline. Meandering between the islands gives the loch an enclosed feeling, before you emerge onto a vast stretch of open water shimmering for miles. This area really lends itself to an overnight trip, with many of the islands having idyllic camping spots.

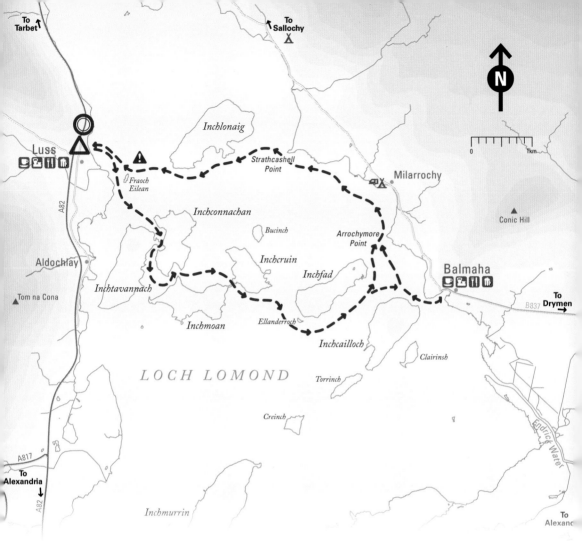

This trip starts in the picturesque tourist hotspot of Luss. Originally built as housing for the Colquhoun estate, this area quickly gained interest as pilgrims came to pay their respects to St Kessog. This Irish saint built a monastery on Inchtavannach, whose name is derived from the Gaelic for Island of the Monk's House.

Each island has a history attached to it, and the most unusual on this trip is surely Inchconnachan. Lady Colquhoun was known, among other things, for her love of exotic animals. In the 1940s she decided one of these species should come with her to her holiday home on the island. The wallabies she took with her flourished on the island and produced a thriving population. Years of inbreeding and a cull several years ago have made the remaining marsupials much more shy, but you can still catch glimpses of them bouncing through the undergrowth.

Inchmoan and Inchcruin are separated by a narrow channel, often shallow enough to walk between, known as The Geggles. The former was a hotspot for peat harvesting to heat the houses in Luss, so it's no surprise that the Inchmoan whiskey sold by the Loch Lomond Distillery is one of their peatier options. Inchcruin, meaning round island, housed an 18th century institute for the insane.

Bucinch and Ceardach are two smaller islands to the north-east of Inchcruin. Bucinch's rocky terrain and single high point make it the ideal home of the goat, from which the name is derived, although none now remain on the island. Meanwhile Ceardach, or the Tinker's Island, was the location of an iron age furnace. It also has a small natural harbour and on calm days makes for a spectacular lunch spot.

Inchfad, to the east of the loch, was originally the location of illicit whiskey distillation and distribution. This was cracked down on however, and the distilleries shut. They were reopened again, albeit legally this time, and operated until the mid-19th century. It now has an operational farm and two permanent residents.

At the northern end of the island group, Fraoch Eilean was the site of Luss Prison and Inchlonaig has a healthy population of yew trees, originally planted in 1300 by Robert the Bruce. He needed supple wood to make bows for his archers and the wood from Inchlonaig was used at the battle of Bannockburn in 1314.

Trip overview

Parking at Luss can be difficult as it gets extremely busy in the summer months. If you do manage to get parked at Luss, the village shop sells a selection of hot and cold filled rolls as well as drinks, and many trips on Loch Lomond have started with breakfast here.

The pier at Luss is a busy place, with boats coming and going regularly. In the summer months it is a popular diving platform for youngsters. It's worth giving the pier a wide berth to avoid picking up unwanted passengers.

Between Inchlonaig and Fraoch Eilean is almost a kilometre of open water. Northerly winds can create serious fetch here and turn this crossing into a difficult, even dangerous stretch of the trip. In this instance, we would recommend turning and heading toward Milarrochy and retracing your steps across the island chain.

This trip can effortlessly be turned into an easy overnight camping adventure as there are many good camping places on the islands.

The route

Launching at Luss beach, head south along the shore.

Cross to Inchtavannach to the north-west point and follow the northern shore to the narrows between here and Inchconnachan. It is easy to become distracted at this point as you watch red deer bound down the shores of Inchtavannach, the deer having swum here from the mainland. Enjoy this sheltered and magical place, but keep half an eye out for boats; the cruisers come down this channel, their passage laid out by cardinal marks.

Leaving the narrows you come to a bay between the three islands. Head eastward between Inchconnachan and Inchmoan. If you have the time and are keen to explore a ruined castle then visit on Inchgalbraith, just south-west of Inchmoan.

Paddle east along the north coast of Inchmoan, then through The Geggles and along the south coast of Inchcruin. Alternatively head north and then around this island clockwise and you can pop over to Bucinch and Ceardach. From Inchcruin cross to Inchfad. The usual crossing here would be past the cardinal marks at the south-east of Inchcruin.

From Inchfad you head east toward Arrochymore Point and here you make a decision. The route described heads north to Milarrochy, then Strathcashell Point. For those who want a lunch stop or a drink at this point, a quick kilometre south and you'll find yourself in Balmaha. If you are short on time you could drop a car in Milarrochy and do this as a one way trip from Luss.

Assuming you've decided to go north, follow the east shore to Strathcashell Point. For those who want to make this an overnight trip, but who aren't keen on island camping, there is Sallochy just a couple of kilometres north of here. This is an organised campsite and you need to book in advance.

Cross from Strathcashell Point to Inchlonaig and follow the southern shore. This is another sizable island, worth exploring and wandering through the yew trees. The crossing from Inchlonaig to Fraoch Eilean is a long stretch of open water and should only be undertaken if you're certain the conditions are favourable. From Fraoch Eilean it's a quick hop back over the Luss to finish the journey.

3 Northern Circuit

Get on / off	NN 321 045
Time required	6+ hours
Distance	25km
Parking / shuttle	NN 321 045

Introduction

Tarbet, where this trip starts, gains its name from the Gaelic word for isthmus. This narrow strip between Loch Lomond and Loch Long was the launching spot for the Viking pillaging raids on the loch. You can recreate this trip, minus the theft, as a multi day adventure (see page 127).

The Tarbet Isle, just off the shore to the north of the village, has also been known as the 'Honeymoon Isle'. The story goes that newlyweds were sent here to live together in solitude for a week. This was a test of their marital strength and were they still in the 'honeymoon period' come the end of the week it was a sign the marriage was destined to last.

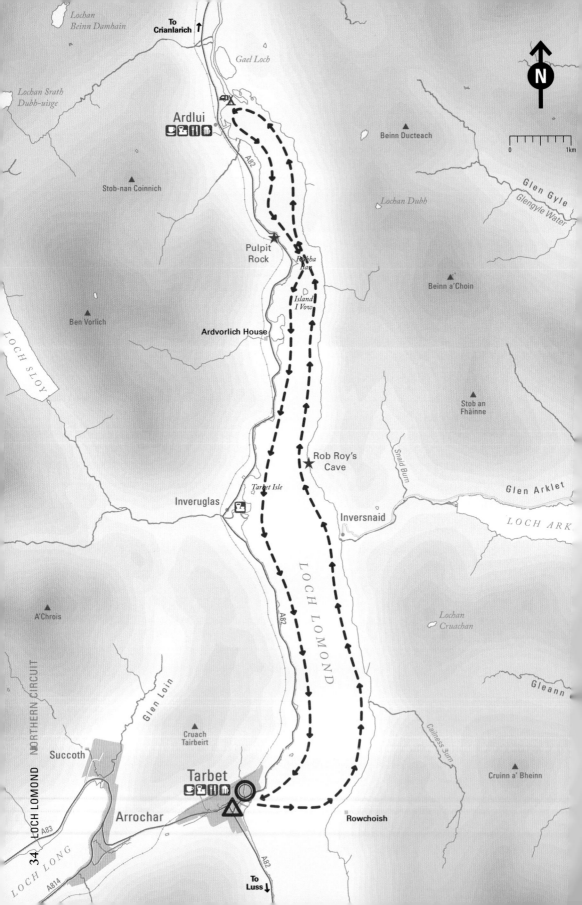

N

0   1km

LOCH LOMOND NORTHERN CIRCUIT

To
Crianlarich

Lochan
Beinn Damhain

Gael Loch

Lochan Srath
Dubh-uisge

Ardlui

A82

Beinn Ducteach

Stob-nan Coinnich

Lochan Dubh

LOCH SLOY

Ben Vorlich

Pulpit
Rock

Robha
Ban

Island
I Vow

Beinn a'Choin

Glen Gyle

Glengyle Water

Ardvorlich House

Stob an
Fhàinne

Rob Roy's
Cave

Glen Arklet

Inveruglas

Tarbet Isle

Inversnaid

LOCH ARK

A'Chrois

LOCH LOMOND

Lochan
Cruachan

Snaid Burn

A82

Gleann

Glen Loin

Cruach
Tairbeirt

Cruinn a' Bheinn

Succoth

Tarbet

Cailness Burn

A83

Arrochar

Rowchoish

LOCH LONG

A814

A82

To
Luss

The Inversnaid Hotel sits across from Inveruglas, and ferries regularly cross here with day visitors. This is a popular way of walking some of the less accessible hills to the north east of Loch Lomond.

Further north, Island I Vow is the seat of the Clan Macfarlane, where they fled after the ever-popular Oliver Cromwell destroyed their old one on the Inveruglas Isle. The remains of this castle on Island I Vow are still there and while it may not get the same rave reviews it did in 1710; "a pretty good house with gardens", it's worth a visit while you're there.

On the western shore, a couple of kilometres short of Ardlui, is the Pulpit Rock. Clach nan Tarbh (the stone of the bulls) allegedly landed here; it fell from Stuc na Nighinn after an almighty fight between two bulls. In 1825 the rock had a giant hole blasted into it to accommodate the minister, who used this venue for his sermons. It was used regularly for 75 years until a church was opened just up the road in Ardlui.

At the head of the loch, the River Falloch enters. This can be paddled upstream as far as Beinglas Farm at Inverarnan. Here you will find the Drovers Inn, frequented in his time by cattle rustler extraordinaire Rob Roy. This pub is notable for its stuffed bear in the entrance.

Trip overview

Often overlooked in favour of paddling in the south, the northern end of the loch is enclosed by highland mountains, giving it an almost fjord-like feel. With the A82 on one side and the traffic of the west highland way on the other, this is a highly accessible journey. Don't be put off by the thought of all this traffic though, once you're on the water this journey can still feel as remote as you want it to. Waving tourists on passing boats are likely to be the only other people you see as you make your way alone this stretch of water.

Wind often funnels between the hillsides and waves can crash down this northern end. Sections of this trip can be quite committing. There are generally stoppings points in an emergency, but although the A82 follows the west side closely the steep banks and road traffic make egress quite difficult. The eastern shore's only road access is at Inversnaid.

The route

Starting at Tarbet, this trip can be completed in either direction. It's best to see what the weather is doing and decide on the day.

Assuming you're heading anti-clockwise, cross the loch toward Rowchoish. Keep the shore on your right-hand side and paddle north to Inversnaid Hotel where an impressive waterfall crashes into the loch. About a kilometre north of here you will find Rob Roy's cave, where both he and Robert the Bruce allegedly sheltered (separately, they were born several hundred years apart).

Keep heading north until you reach the head of the loch around six kilometres later. Either explore up the lower reaches of the Falloch or keep going round toward Ardlui. Both of these options give you opportunities for a lunch stop in a pub or just on the shore with a view.

This is where the journey heads back south. Just past Rubha Ban, cross to Island I Vow if you want to explore the remains of the Mafarlane Castle. Keep moving south past Ardvorlich and Inveruglas, being careful to avoid the ferries which cross from here.

As you get back towards Tarbet, take a final stop at the Tarbet Isle. If you're with your loved one, why not revisit old traditions and see how you cope with the solitude, although a week may be a bit much!

A quick kilometre back to Tarbet and you have the opportunity to visit the tea rooms before heading off home.

4 Endrick Water

Get on / off	NS 472 874 / NS 419 909
Time required	1–3 hours
Distance	11km
Parking / shuttle	NS 472 875 / 420 909
Optimum water level	Fine at most levels, can get shallow in particularly dry spells.
Grade	1

Introduction

The river known as the Endrick Water starts life as two small burns, the Burnfoot Burn on the Gargunnock hills, and the Backside Burn on the Fintry hills. These combine and flow for kilometres through foothills and small towns before passing under the old military bridge near Drymen, where our trip starts.

This bridge was built originally in the 1700s as a crossing for the military road that would later become the A811, but underwent major reconstruction in the early 1900s. The remains of a motte-and-bailey castle can still be seen nearby, a fortification intended to

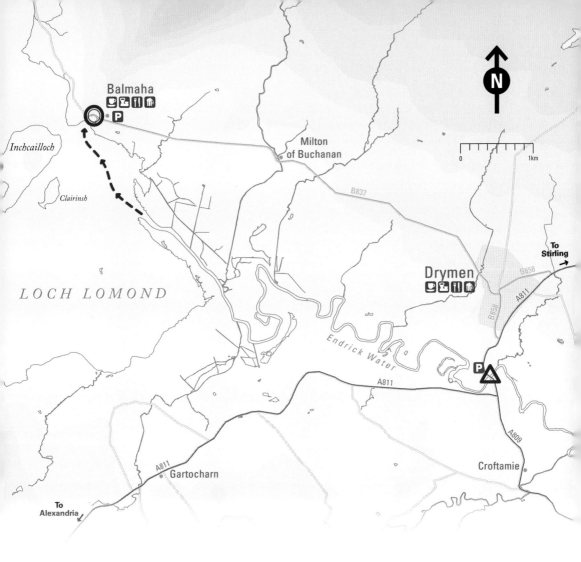

protect the crossing to the highlands. The Clachan, a pub up in Drymen, also dates back to these medieval times, boasting a license originating in 1734.

In the 1800s and 1900s, Drymen became a popular stopover for the drovers as they came down from the north, looking to sell their cattle in larger towns and cities.

Trip overview

Access is from the north side of the bridge; there is a stopping point on the left-hand side of the road with enough room for one car. Access the field here and shuttle other vehicles either to the end point, or the larger car park up in Drymen itself.

A gentle, meandering river, this is perfect for introducing beginners to moving water or as an elongation of the Beautiful South route on Loch Lomond. From the end of the river it's a short, sandy stretch of shoreline to Balmaha where you join the route on page 25.

This river is a popular spot for fishermen. Take care as you move downstream and re-member to be courteous as you pass them.

The section above Drymen Bridge has been paddled, but unless there has been sig-nificant rainfall it is perhaps best described as a walk with a boat, rather than a paddle. Among the shallow rapids are some weirs which create tricky features at some levels.

The route

Head downstream from Drymen Bridge, following the many meanders as the river carries you downstream. There are no rapids to speak of, just sections of gentle flow. Stay aware as you round bends, not just for fishermen, but for the flow pushing you into the banks on the outside of the corners.

As you reach Loch Lomond, the banks open up and you are paddling through sand-banks. Make sure you stay in the deeper sections of the river here otherwise you can quickly find yourself high and dry!

This section of Loch Lomond is extremely popular with wading birds and you will often see all sorts of birdlife here, including the popular and shrill oystercatcher.

Once you emerge onto Loch Lomond, head north to Balmaha. You can egress here, or further north at Milarrochy, or continue on the route for the Beautiful South.

5 River Falloch

Get on / off	NN 337 208 / NN 320 198
Time required	1–3 hours
Distance	3–11km
Parking / shuttle	NN 334 207 / NN 320 198
Optimum Water Level	0.8m+ the river runs, 1.0m–1.2m is optimum, above 1.2m most rapids go up a grade.
Grade	4/5

Introduction

A proper Scottish white-water classic. This river sits close to the top of 'must do' rivers in the country for experienced white-water paddlers.

Paddling apart, this is still a commonly visited attraction. Directly off the A82 as you drive north between Glasgow and the highlands it draws crowds in the summer who love nothing more than a chance to photograph a kayaker going over the falls. There is also a jumping platform here, so be sure the pool at the bottom is clear before paddling it.

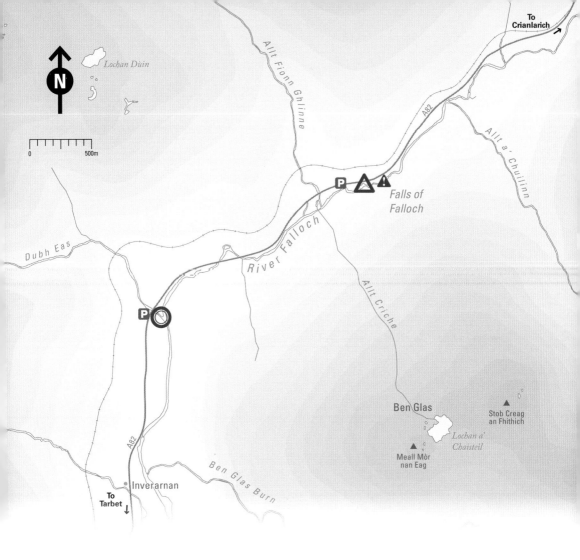

For those with an interest in history, the falls are sometimes referred to as Rob Roy's bathtub; when he wasn't busy stealing cows, he could be found sending backflips off the top drop (not verified).

At the bottom of the river are the remains of the Inverarnan Canal. This was built as access for pleasure steamers which carried tourists up Loch Lomond to the Drovers Arms at Inverarnan. At the time this was not only a pub and accommodation, but also a stagecoach stop, allowing passengers to continue their travel into the highlands.

Trip overview

The car park for the Falls of Falloch is clearly signposted in either direction as you drive between Inverarnan and Crianlarich and from here it's just a short walk to the falls.

The Falls of Falloch is a park and huck delight! These 10-metre falls are probably the second most photographed in Scotland, by paddlers at least. There's even a viewing gallery.

Below the falls is the classic section of grade 4/5 river, including some notable rapids. This is usually run as it drops, rather than rises, and as it drops from a metre to 0.8 on the SEPA gauge is apparently the ideal level for a first timer on this river. This river swells quickly on the way up, and many experienced paddlers have climbed out of a swelling Falloch.

The route

It's up to you whether you choose to run the falls or get-in below and run the river. The falls themselves are run river right and to get-on above them you follow the tourist path from the Falls of Falloch car park to the viewing platform. Just before the metal walkway, climb up a muddy embankment on your left which takes you to the A82. There is a short (10m) track beside the road, then you climb back over the fence and follow the track back to the river. The lead into the falls has caught people out before and has some tricky diagonal features which can be retentive at some river levels.

If you don't fancy running the falls, slide into the pool below to paddle the lower. Some straightforward rapids lead to a grade 4 bend. Below this is more grade 3 and 4 rapids leading to the Seven Dwarfs (grade 5). These seven drops can be inspected from river left. The rapid under the A82 bridge forms a nasty hole.

Further downstream is Twist and Shout (grade 4), a sizeable drop with sticky holes which can be inspected from the big rock in the middle of the river. The final drop should be run over the slabs on the left to avoid the rocks in the main flow.

Egress either at NN 320 198 or paddle the flat water down to Loch Lomond.

Upper Falloch

The lesser run Upper Falloch is a grade 4 section above the falls, with some features and drops worth inspecting before they are run. We aren't going to cover this in too much detail, but if the lower is looking a bit too sporty, the upper can be a good option if you're determined to paddle on the Falloch. Access is NN 369 238, a lay-by off the A82 near Crianlarich, and you egress at Derrydarroch Farm (NN 352 218), just before the falls. Usually if you're running the upper, the falls are going to be pretty meaty, so even if you intend to run them it's worth jumping out for a look.

6 Luss Water

Get on / off	NS 326 940 / NS 356 928
Time required	3+ hours (lots of inspecting and possible portaging)
Distance	4km
Parking / shuttle	NS 326 940 / NS 356 931
Optimum water level	0.9+
Grade	3/4(5)

Introduction

The village of Luss is one of the most popular tourist destinations around Loch Lomond; nevertheless once you head up the glen you quickly leave the crowds behind. As you reach the top of the hill and approach the get-on for the river, be sure to turn around and enjoy a view of the island chain which very few people see.

At the end of this river are the remnants of Luss slate quarry and much of the housing in modern day Luss was built to accommodate the workers.

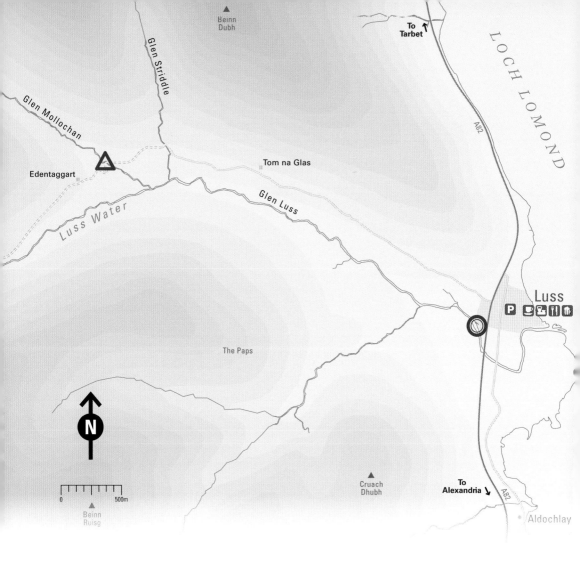

The short walk through the woods after you get off the river includes a section of the Glen Luss Faerie Trail, a magical walk for youngsters who can see doorways to faery houses and make wishes as they walk around the woods.

Trip overview

The get-on is up Glen Luss, off the A82. As you approach Edentaggart there is a bridge crossing the Mollochan Burn; this is the get-on and there is space for a single vehicle here. If you want to avoid the burn itself, where some of the narrower, more difficult drops are, there's a turning point just before this bridge. This is a no parking area, so we recommend you use it to drop off your kit and then park elsewhere further down the glen.

Despite its accessibility, the Luss is rarely paddled. It's a narrow, relatively committing run from the Mollochan Burn to Loch Lomond. Generally a grade 4, with some drops

warranting inspection and portage, there is potential to find trees at any turn. This isn't a river to bowl around any blind bends on or to drop hopefully into a rapid, but a slower trip requiring regular scouting.

The route

Mollochan Burn is very narrow and prone to overhanging; and maybe even fallen trees. This lead-in offers no real warm-up before some serious rapids, including a difficult double drop toward the end, which is worth inspecting / portaging river left.

Once onto the Luss itself you will find good sections of grade 4, the grade dropping slowly as you work your way downstream. Some of the drops and longer rapids require inspection and may be a portage, mainly because of trees.

Around the halfway mark you'll come across the Falls of Luss, a very steep, narrow, and almost definitely tree-filled drop. The rapid above is an easy enough right-hand bend, but it feels more gorgey as you get towards it. There are eddies above the falls; just make sure you don't miss them, as this is the last chance to run away or inspect.

Below the falls the river becomes easier but still very enjoyable, dropping a grade to grade 3. Read and run this section but stay awake for blockages. The last couple of drops through the old slate mine are a fun way to finish the run. The weir at the end of this mine is a potential get-out, or head all the way to Loch Lomond. The weir itself can be a bit messy, but is an easy enough portage.

7 River Leven

Get on / off:	NS 386 823 / NS 393 754
Time required:	3+ hours (lots of inspecting and possible portaging)
Distance:	8km
Parking / shuttle:	NS 386 823 / NS 393 754
Optimum water level:	0.9+
Grade:	1

Introduction

From the Gaelic for Elm Water, as per the crest of the Earl of Lennox, this river was historically a key route for the industry in Glasgow. It flows gently from Loch Lomond to the Clyde and is where the Vikings left Loch Lomond after their pillaging exploits in the area. This trip finishes in Dumbarton, the capital of the ancient Kingdom of Strathclyde, more recently the home of shipyards.

The barrage at the head of the river was built to control flooding on the river and maintain water levels in Loch Lomond. Downstream of here are the old rail yards which

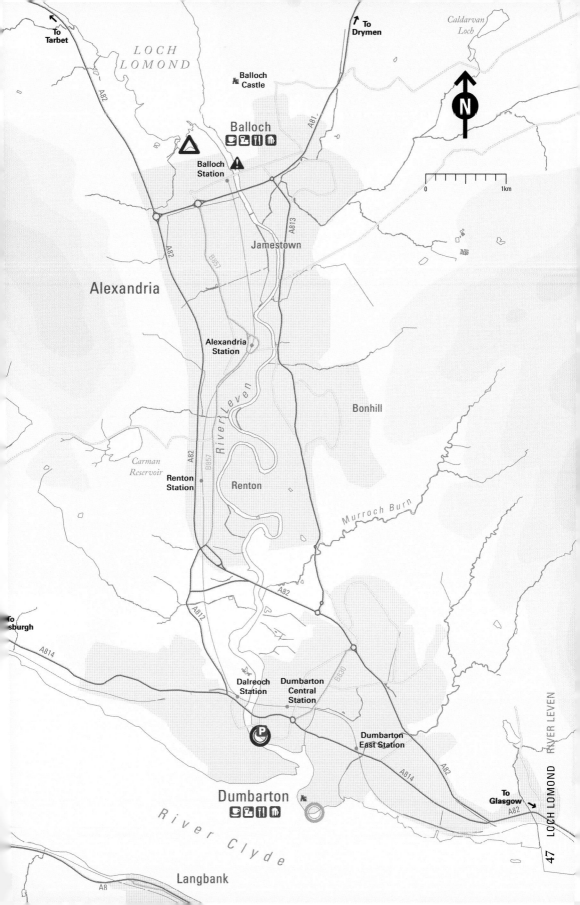

To Tarbet

LOCH LOMOND

Balloch Castle

Caldarvan Loch

N

0 ——————— 1km

A82

A81

To Drymen

Balloch

Balloch Station

Jamestown

A813

Alexandria

B857

Alexandria Station

Carman Reservoir

Renton Station

Renton

A82

B857

River Leven

Bonhill

Murroch Burn

To ...sburgh

A814

A812

A82

B830

Dalreoch Station

Dumbarton Central Station

Dumbarton East Station

A814

A82

P

Dumbarton

RIVER LEVEN

LOCH LOMOND

To Glasgow

A82

47

River Clyde

Langbank

A8

once served large industrial areas, now housing the Loch Lomond Brewery and used to store whiskey casks.

Trip overview

A gently flowing river which is a throwback to the industrial era. You wind your way through the open countryside and the town of Dumbarton. This is a popular beginners' river and can also be combined easily with other routes, such as the Endrick Water or the Beautiful South to make for a longer paddle.

The route

Leave Drumkinnon Bay and follow the shore round past the *Maid of the Loch* and onto the river.

Just after you get into the river and pass through the marina, you will come to the barrage. Portage this on the right hand side.

The river meanders its way down to Dumbarton through a mixture of countryside and historic industry. The last couple of rapids here depend largely on whether the tide is in on the Clyde, ranging from low grade 2 to flat water.

There is a public slip at the council offices to serve as egress; alternatively continue to Dumbarton Castle out on the Firth of Clyde. It is worth checking the tide times as at low tide the beach is deep sandy mud.

Scottish Maritime Museum

Visit the Scottish Maritime Museum in Dumbarton after you finish for an insight into the industrial past of the area you've just paddled through.

The calm of the morning \ Photo: PaddleMore

THE TROSSACHS

Winter in the Trossachs \ Photo PaddleMore

The Trossachs

When the name 'Trossachs' (Na Tròisechan) first came into common use, it referred only to a small wooded glen in the middle of the modern day area. Often described as the 'highlands in miniature', the Trossachs is an uncommonly beautiful, varied landscape. Rising steeply from the eastern shores of Loch Lomond, the area comprises some eight navigable lochs and Scotland's only natural 'lake'. The Trossachs slope down from here into more lowland areas and the boundary ends by Callander, and further south the Lake of Menteith. From the boundary the hills mellow and you're just a stone's throw from Stirling, historic capital of Scotland (Robert the Bruce held a parliament there in 1326), which binds the lowlands and highlands together.

A handful of towns in the area draw the majority of the crowds. Callander on the eastern boundary is a popular tourist destination and the start of the River Teith. Meanwhile Aberfoyle, near Loch Ard, sees a fair share of holidaymakers and is the starting point for a walk up Doon Hill. A renowned hotspot in folklore for 'fae' (fairies), the tree at the top of the hill is seen as the gateway to their kingdom.

OPEN WATER

8 Three Lochs Forest Drive

9 Loch Venachar

10 Loch Arklet

11 Loch Ard

12 Loch Katrine

13 Loch Chon

14 Lake of Menteith

RIVERS

15 River Teith – Easy WW Grade 1/2

16 The Black Water

Sunset in the Trossachs \ Photo PaddleMore

Loch Achray (about to head down Black Water) \ Photo Zoe Niven

8 Three Lochs Forest Drive

Introduction

The forest drive winds its way slowly downhill from the A821, two miles north of Aberfoyle, and is opened daily. Don't forget to take some coins to pay the toll at the start of this road which, at the time of writing, is just a couple of pounds. This off-road trail passes three lochs between the Duke's Pass, where it starts, and finishes at the Loch Achray Campsite, perfect for a weekend of camping and getting the family out on the water. Alternative camping is available at Loch Drunkie.

For these three small lochs, we haven't included a route. They are small bodies of water which are generally very sheltered, and as such it felt unnecessary to dictate a direction. They are all suitable for families, or a short splash around on the water, or a leisurely paddle and exploration.

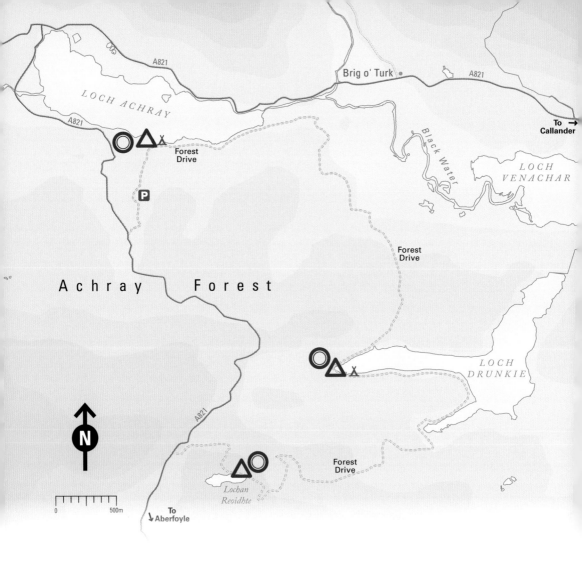

LOCHAN REOIDHTE

Get on / off	NN 524 035
Time required	Less than 1 hour
Distance	600m
Parking / shuttle	NN 524 035

The first and smallest of the three, this lochan might not register high on the radar for most, but easy access and picturesque location may make it the perfect place for a family afternoon in the sunshine. This is the first piece of water you come across on the Three Lochs Forest Drive and is the top of the watershed which flows down into Loch Achray and beyond.

LOCH DRUNKIE

Get on / off	NN 532 043
Time required	1–3 hours
Distance	4km
Parking / shuttle	NN 532 043

Another small loch and very rarely visited, Loch Drunkie is considerably larger than Lochan Reoidht, but still a small body of water. It's a great place for a first day trip. The hills around the loch shelter it from almost any wind and the secluded nature of the loch means you will most likely have it all to yourselves. At the northern end there is a man-made wall, the holes and crevices of which house adders, often seen basking in the sunshine.

There are a number of laybys along the forest drive which can be used to access Loch Drunkie, but generally it would be accessed either at the end of the southern arm, or the Loch Drunkie car park at the western tip. Be sure to explore all the arms and bays on the loch, there are many stunning pieces of forest right off the water and endless spots for picnics. There are trails all round the loch too, and the Pine Ridge trail, from the Loch Drunkie car park is a 1.5km trail which gets you up onto the hills, giving you incredible views over the loch, an option for those who want to combine paddling and walking

LOCH ACHRAY

Get on / off	NN 515 061
Time required	1–3 hours
Distance	6km
Parking / shuttle	NN 514 057

Although larger than Lochan Reoidhte and Loch Drunkie, it's still considered a small loch. The mist, which often hangs on the loch in the morning, gives it the feeling of a much larger body of water and shrouds the banks. Once this clears, the usually still surface reflects Ben Venue and Ben A'an beautifully, a photographer's dream. There are a number of bays to explore and a couple of small islands on the loch. James 'Beg' Stewart, son of James the Fat, once had a hunting lodge on the island at the west end, which he allegedly retreated to at the slightest hint of danger to himself.

At the east end of the loch, the Black Water flows out toward Loch Venachar. The outflow is hard to see initially, obscured by forest. You can often delve slightly into this river and then paddle back out, but be careful not to be caught out by the flow.

Loch Achray is accessible toward the end of the Forest Drive, or you can park in the main car park for the Loch Achray Campsite and walk your boat the few hundred metres to the water's edge. Alternatively there are car parks for Ben Venue and Ben A'an off the A821 which can also be used.

Loch Achray is probably most commonly paddled as the start of a day trip down to Loch Venachar, via the Black Water.

9 Loch Venachar

Get on / off	NN 598 061
Time required	1–3 hours
Distance	12km
Parking / shuttle	NN 598 060

Introduction

Sheltered by the Menteith hills to the south and Ben Ledi to the north, this six kilometre loch often remains relatively calm when it's blowing a hooley everywhere else. Loch Venachar sits in the bottom of a glaciated valley, and is part of the water network which used to bring drinking water from Loch Katrine down to Glasgow. With newer technology changing the way water is transported, the old dams have been repurposed as a flood defence for Callander and Stirling.

Queen Victoria visited Loch Venachar in 1896 and stayed at Invertrossachs, a small hamlet on the southern shore where fortress-like buildings stand sentinel over the loch.

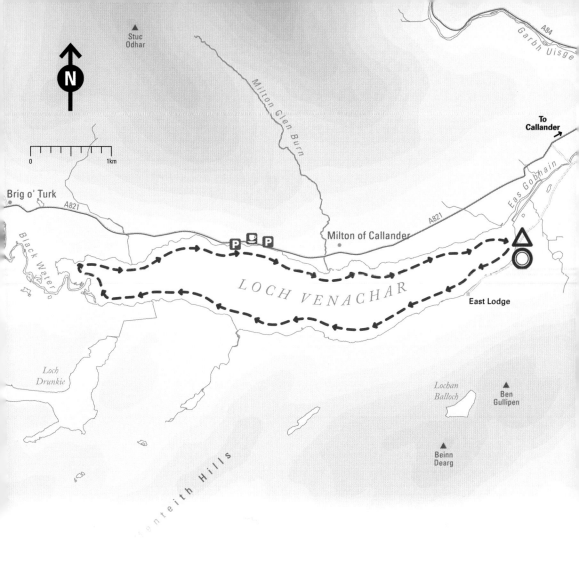

Also on this shore are a popular Scout campsite, a sailing club and the Ripple Retreat, a beautiful facility which allows respite for families of young cancer patients.

Trip overview

Follow the road to Invertrossachs from Callander until you reach the small National Trust Park car park at the eastern end of Loch Venachar next to the waterworks. Alternatively access from the northern shore at one of the two picnic spots on your left, after Milton of Callander.

Loch Venachar is relatively small and generally has quite calm water. The road follows the northern shore, while to the south there is either track or trail along most of the loch. Because this loch is often sheltered it can be a good place to get a feel for paddling further from shore, but this is wind dependent.

The route

Set off from the car park on the eastern shores, taking care as you do so. The old water-works occasionally draw some flow and on otherwise calm days can catch people out.

Head westward along the southern shore. You soon pass impressive houses high up on the lochside, and before long you come to the sailing club. Take care here, especially on weekends when there may be races or events on the water. As you pass the Invertrossachs campsite further along the shore, you're likely to see, in the summer months, canoes and bell boats full of scouts exploring the water.

As you reach the west end of the loch, there are a number of places on the south shore to stop in the forest. A track follows most of the shoreline and here it is close to the water, separated by small clearings in the forest, an idyllic place for lunch if the midges allow.

The Black Water flows into the west end of Loch Venachar, with the lower reaches being a mainly deep, gentle flow. You can paddle part way up this and are likely to see a wide array of birdlife in the trees and high banks of the river before turning around and allowing the flow to wash you back into the loch.

Following the northern shore now, the more open landscape will treat you to views around the hillside and farmland. Animals regularly come down to the water's edge to drink and you can get closer here to a highland cow than they usually allow on land.

A little further on you will pass Milton of Callander, a perfect spot to stop for a coffee or some lunch and visit the art gallery. The remainder of the trip along the north shore continues much the same and before you know it you will find yourself at the waterworks. Again, take care around any inflow as you pass them before heading back to the car park.

Kelpies

Don't get eaten by the kelpies here. These shape shifting spirits lure unsuspecting water users to their doom!

The Kelpie is the most common of the Scottish water spirits and stories of these shapeshifting beasts can be found throughout Celtic folklore.

Living in large bodies of water, the kelpies, whose normal form is that of a large black horse, would also often poorly disguise themselves as humans with water weeds as hair and try to tempt solitary travellers to their watery grave.

10 Loch Arklet

Get on / off	NN 397 096
Time required	1–3 hours
Distance	10km
Parking / shuttle	NN 397 096

Introduction

Loch Arklet is the highest loch in the Trossachs and is the top of the chain of lochs in the Glasgow Corporation Water Work System. In the early 20th century, a dam was erected at the west end to redirect the outflow and keep Loch Katrine topped up.

In 1693, Rob Roy MacGregor was married to Mary MacGregor of Comar at Corrie Arklet farm, on the Northern shore. Mary was born locally, at Leny Farm on the shores of the Balvaig.

If you're looking for somewhere to stay around here, or want to grab something to eat either before launching or halfway through the day, Inversnaid bunkhouse is just off the west end of the loch, a couple of hundred metres further down the road than the end of the water.

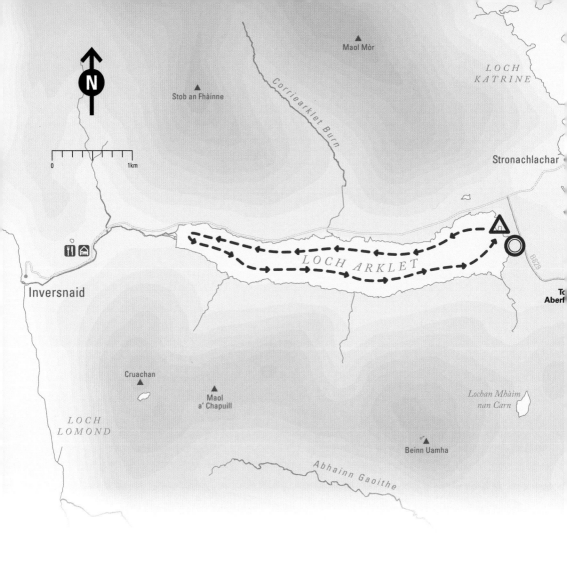

Trip overview

There is limited parking and access for this loch. At the eastern end there is parking for several vehicles and a short walk down a track brings you to the edge of the loch. Take care launching here as you are close to the water works, which can have a slight inflow and are best avoided.

Often this loch is sheltered by the surrounding hills, but certain wind directions funnel through here and can wreak havoc even on such a small body of water. Loch Arklet can be subject to some large waves and can be a great place to practise some open-water paddling skills in tricky conditions.

This loch is often part of a longer trip and links Loch Lomond to Loch Katrine and there are a number of options for camping on the southern shore, including an old farmstead at Corrieachan.

The route

Along the north shore you follow the course of the road which runs east to west between Loch Katrine and Loch Lomond. The northern shore feels more open and can be more susceptible to winds which blow through here. Unlike the south side here, there is a small relief before the hills start. The views over the southern shore and the Corbetts behind make this shore well worth a paddle, but most of the points of interest are on the southern shores of this loch.

On your return, the southern shore climbs steeply toward a number of hills including Beinn Uamha, which despite its small stature gives incredible views over the Trossachs. There are plenty of stopping points on this shore for breaks as you make your way back along toward the waterworks.

Corbetts

Corbetts are mountains in Scotland which range between 2500ft (762m) and 3000ft (914m). To be considered a true Corbett, there must be 500ft (152m) of vertical descent on all sides of the summit.

Feral goats roam the shores between Loch Arklet and Loch Lomond, where these master mountaineers can be seen picking their way between the rocks as they search for food.

Boating with Mum \ Photo Phil Robinson

11 Loch Ard

Get on / off	NN 453 021
Time required	3+ hours
Distance	13km
Parking / shuttle	NN 453 021

Introduction

Situated just to the west of Aberfoyle, Loch Ard is a popular area for walking and cycling as well as paddling. Despite the popularity of the forests surrounding it, the loch itself feels secluded and is a welcome escape from the crowds which gather in Aberfoyle in the summer months. The popular tourist town is full of shops and cafés, and the butchers, just a short walk from the main car park in town, sell hot rolls and fantastic pies. It's a perfect place to stock up for a picnic on Eilean Gorm, the island on Loch Ard.

Many of the sculptures which make up the Loch Ard sculpture trail are visible from the water as you paddle down the southern shores. In fact, one of them is on the loch itself. Keep an eye out as you paddle for these impressive pieces of artwork.

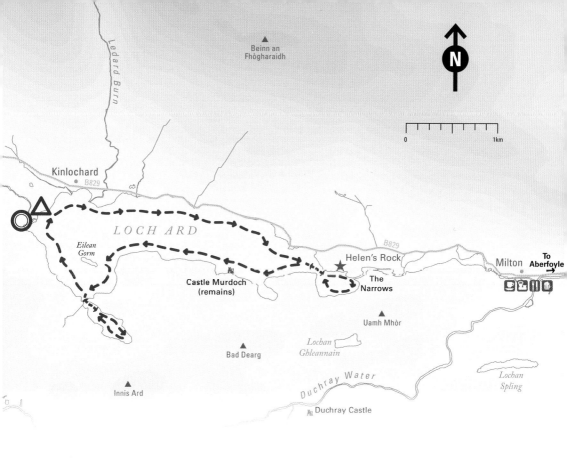

Castle Murdoch, on an island halfway along the southern shore, was built by the Duke of Albany, a cousin of King James I, in 1425. There is also evidence of crannogs on the loch.

In World War Two an armed launch patrolled these waters, deterring German seaplanes from bombing the ammunition dump on the shores. Further back in history, Victorian gentry floated musicians on the loch as they sailed around to increase the ambience around the islands. They would often base themselves around Helen's Rock, at the east end of the loch, where Helen MacGregor made use of an echo which reverberated around the water to throw off pursuers who were following Rob Roy to one of his many caves (which can still be found at the west end).

Crannogs

These houses built on lochs throughout Scotland are usually in the form of a man-made island, or a roundhouse built on piles driven deep into the loch bed. The earliest recorded findings of these are around 5,000 years old!

Trip overview

The main parking, at the Kinlochard Community Centre at the west end of the loch, requests a donation toward the upkeep. There is a jetty here and plenty of space to kit up before getting on the water. Alternatively, turn off the B829 at Milton and park just south of the small lochan to the east of Loch Ard.

This sub-lochan is attached to Loch Ard via a narrow channel, usually easily navigable in both directions. Heavy rain however can generate some flow and it can be tricky to paddle up. Loch Ard is generally quite sheltered, and being a small body of water, the fetch doesn't build the waves like it can on some larger lochs. In the evenings, this loch is often treated to incredible sunsets over the smaller hills to the west and is often chosen for a first overnight trip. Remember that the camping on the shores is within the camping management zone and should be booked first.

The route

From the western end of the loch, follow along the north shore. The road here is close to the water's edge, and you can see your whole trip laid out ahead of you. As you reach the east end of the loch, you may decide to head quickly down the narrows towards Milton. If you do, you will be rewarded with a completely different feeling piece of water. Shallower and with plenty of pond life around the edges, this little lochan attracts plenty of wildlife. For those who park at Milton, join the trip here.

From this lochan, head back up the narrows and out along the southern side of the loch, making sure to delve into all the many bays this loch has on offer. On the southern side of Loch Ard you will find the remains of Castle Murdock, well worth a stop and explore, especially if you have youngsters with you.

Further along this shore you reach a distinct point and the loch turns left. In front of you here is Eilean Gorm, a beautiful island and perfect for camping. Being so close to the shore on three of its four sides, Eilean Gorm is almost always accessible, and more liable to a breeze than the shore, keeping away those pesky midges!

Just south of the island there is a crannog which peeks just above the surface of the water. These historic houses are often no more than ruins. A narrow entrance just past here reveals another bay, calm and hidden, on the south shores of which there is a camping management zone which you can pre-book to stay in if you fancy a bit more shore security than Eilean Gorm offers.

Turning north from here, you can re-visit Eilean Gorm, or visit it for the first time if you missed it, on your way back to Kinlochard.

Shirley Robertson, double Olympic medallist in sailing,

first took to the water on Loch Ard.

12 Loch Katrine

Get on / off	NN 405 103
Time required	3+ hours
Distance	26km
Parking / shuttle	NN 403 102

Introduction

Most famous as the inspiration for The Lady of the Lake, a poem by Sir Walter Scott, after whom the paddle steamer which tours these waters is named. Loch Katrine is the largest loch in the Trossachs. When Queen Victoria visited in 1896, she sailed on the *Sir Walter Scott*, and stayed in a specially built house on the southern shore, as well as down at Loch Venachar. She still sails today (the boat, not Queen Victoria) and is a popular tourist attraction, hundreds of people boarding her each day in the summer (again, for clarity, the boat).

At the head of the loch is Glengyle, birthplace of Rob Roy MacGregor. This area has just a few ramshackle buildings remaining and feels like an innocuous place for such a

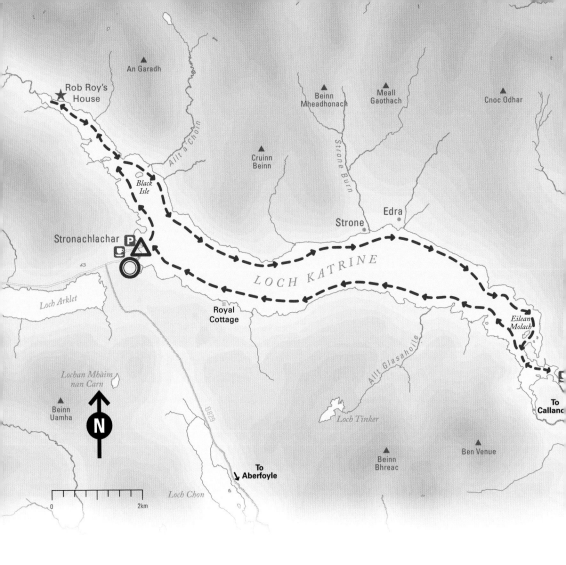

renowned cattle rustler to have been born.

The loch has in times gone by been one of the primary supplies of drinking water for Glasgow. Historically the chain ran all the way down to Loch Venachar, but with modern developments the process is now much more direct.

Trip overview

We recommend parking at Stronachlachar and starting from there. The extra drive takes you away from the car park for the *Sir Walter Scott*, which becomes overcrowded, especially in the summer months. Access is possible at the eastern end at the pay and display car park, but it is sometimes contested and they request you ring ahead. Either way, take care to avoid the steamers. This is more easily managed at Stronachlachar, as you can see them coming a long way off and time your getting on accordingly. This can also be paddled as a linear trip with two vehicles, making for a shorter trip. Choose your start / finish according to prevailing wind conditions and be sure to phone ahead for parking.

Thanks to the altitude of Loch Katrine, it is often windy on the water, and conditions change quickly. On a calm day it may be tempting to head off on an adventure into the more open sections of the loch, but changeable weather and a long fetch can make this a treacherous place to get caught out. We recommend staying to the bays around the edge of the loch, which offer shelter from the wind. To the east of Stronachlachar, the loch for the most part is over a kilometre wide, making this quite a committing trip. You either have to paddle around the loch or commit to a relatively long crossing on open water.

The route

Starting out from Stronachlachar, head north along the shore until you reach the head of the loch. As it narrows out, spurs and small islands protrude from the shore, offering some shelter in windy conditions. Just after rounding the head of the loch you pass Glengyle.

Follow the northern shore and you will come to the Black Isle. This is a great place to hop out for a leg stretch and a wander around the island. Jump back on the water and follow the northern shore further around the obvious crook in the loch. There are countless bays and beaches as you follow the shore along, and if you do end up in the wind you can largely hop from bay to bay until you reach the three small settlements of Strone, Edra and Letter. From here, the lochside is much more open for a couple of kilometres until you reach the pier near Brenachoile Lodge.

This southern end of the loch is worlds apart from the open body of water. It narrows down and becomes more enclosed, the sides get steeper and there are more bays and islands to protect you. The loch really narrows down as you pass Eilean Molach, and the steamers come in and out of the narrows here. If you choose to head all the way in toward the piers then be very careful.

Eilean Molach, however, is a great place for a lunch stop if you are following this trip all the way back to Stronachlachar. From the island, cross to the southern shore and follow it all the way back. Once again, there are many bays and spurs to offer you shelter and to explore, and a few kilometres short of Stronachlachar you will pass the royal cottage and pier where Queen Victoria stayed in 1896.

This trip is subject to wind conditions, and sometimes you may be better off completing it in reverse to have the wind behind you, or alternatively following the same (sheltered) shore in either direction.

© Loch Chon | Photo Charlene McDonald

13 Loch Chon

Get on / off	NN 427 047
Time required	1–3 hours
Distance	5km
Parking / shuttle	NN 427 047

Introduction

Similar to Loch Drunkie, Loch Chon is a small piece of water which is underappreciated within the park, overshadowed as it is by the larger lochs it is so close to. At only 2.5km long and a few hundred metres wide, this loch is often just a spectacle on the way to Loch Katrine, but with beautiful bays, a handful of islands and a rich history in mythology it can be the perfect place for a short trip, even a first overnight for the family.

According to Louis Stott in *Enchantments of the Trossachs* (1992) this loch is home to more fairies than anywhere else in the world. He also writes of Kelpies here. Similar to those on Loch Venachar, these shape shifting spirits haunt the waters and hunt the unwary, their sticky hides not allowing you to get off once you've mounted them.

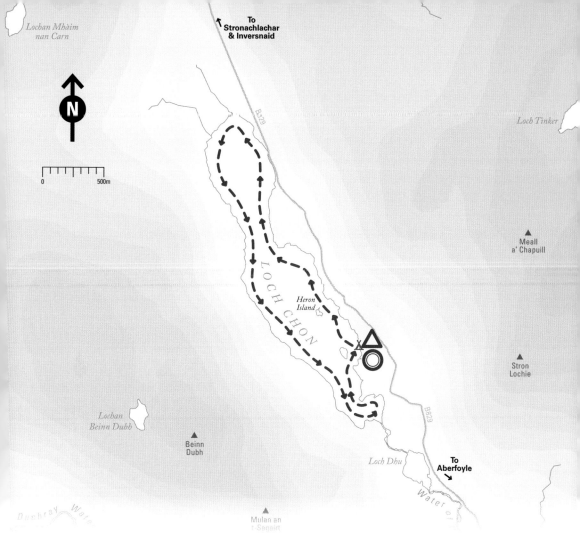

Trip overview

Parking for Loch Chon is just off the B829 as you head north from Loch Ard, west of Aberfoyle. This is where the Loch Chon organised campsite is located and may be busy in the height of summer. There is alternative parking south of here, at NN 428 043, where overnight parking is prohibited. This secondary parking is next to a sheltered and quiet bay, perfect for honing your skills before a short journey.

Loch Chon is situated just to the east of Ben Lomond. It is the most southerly Munro in Scotland, and has a number of smaller hills surrounding it. Footpaths circle the loch and allow for easy access, and there are a number of wild camping spots on the western shores. These are perfect for those looking for a quick and secluded overnight trip but be aware of the Camping Management Zones, active between April and September.

The campsite in the south east of the loch, similarly to Loch Achray, makes for a brilliant family overnight trip, or camping holiday with intermittent splashing around in the summer months.

The route

Launching from the campsite / car park, you are immediately faced with the opportunity to head to one of the countless islands in the National Park. Head north along the east side of the loch toward Heron Island and watch out for these graceful, gangly birds as they wade around the shallows searching for food. These majestic birds can be seen gliding from perch to perch as they maintain their territories. This eastern shore gives you some shelter from any winds which are blowing from Loch Katrine.

Return via the western shores, where generally you should be helped along a little by that breeze you were sheltering from on your route north. Take time to visit the shores and search for fairies as you make your way back to the parking or campsite at the south end.

14 Lake of Menteith

Get on / off	NN 582 010
Time required	1–3 hours
Distance	8km
Parking / shuttle	NN 583 010

Introduction

Believed falsely by many to be the only lake in Scotland, the Lake of Menteith is in fact the only naturally occurring body of fresh water referred to as a lake. There seems to be no consensus on the unusual name; however several potential reasons have been put forward, including 16th century Dutch cartographers mistranslation of 'Laich' meaning low place. As the first people to generally write things down, the English had a lot of say in Scottish names, and referred to every body of water in the Trossachs as lakes. For example the Lake of Loch Chon, ignoring the commonly used Scottish name, Loch Inchmahome (the lake of the island of the home, after the priory on the island), or the fact that loch means lake. They named this body of water after the local town, Menteith. The name Lake Menteith

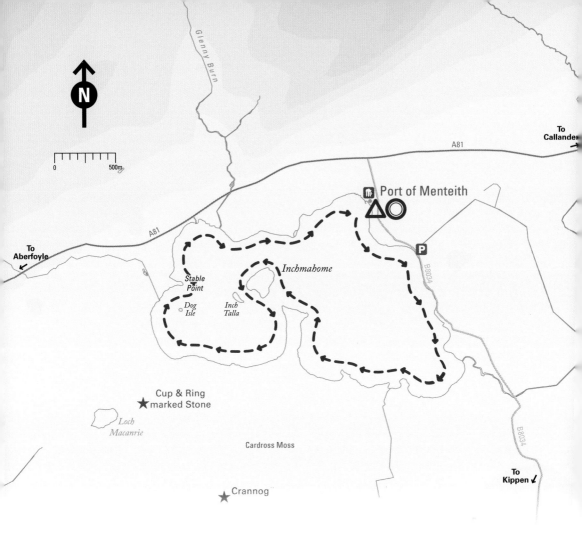

has stuck, and the pub quiz question was born, although if you ever find yourself asked it again, feel free to argue the case for Pressmennan Lake in East Lothian.

The priory on Inchmahome was once refuge to a young Mary Queen of Scots. In 1547 the young Queen was brought to the priory at the age of four for roughly three weeks, while her right to the throne was being challenged, prior to her move to Dumbarton Castle and then onto France in 1548.

Inch Talla, just west of Inchmahome, is taken up almost entirely by the remains of a castle, built for the Earl of Menteith, originally built out of material taken from the priory itself.

The Earl of Menteith had kennels on the Dog Isle, a small circular island just to the south-west of Inch Talla. The unusually uniform shape of this isle is due to it being the site of an ancient crannog. It was one of four crannogs on the loch: 'The Port of Menteith

Crannog' near the modern day town, 'Lochend Crannog' in the south-east, 'Inchmahome Crannog' at the northern end of the island, and the 'Dog Isle Crannog'.

There is evidence of a fifth, 'The Black Loch Crannog'. This site is now almost a kilometre from the lake, hardly the site for a water-based building. In fact, there used to be a small body of water here, The Black Loch, where the crannog was built, but the loch has since drained.

This loch is popular with wreck divers searching for the 'submarine spitfire' crashed by Thomas Hetherington in 1943 while showing off to the girls working the fields beside the lake. At the west end of the lake are some military jetties from when the area was used as an ammunition dump in World War Two.

Trip overview

Park at the small car park in the north east of the loch, just off the B8034. The small lake is almost split into two pieces by a large protrusion from the south. Another small body of water, the lake sits much lower than any of the lochs in the park and is often not subjected to the same sorts of winds as they are.

The route

Leaving the car park, head south along the eastern shore and boundary of the national park, until you reach Lochend House. Now turn east and follow the sweeping bay which takes you to the head of the southern protrusion. It's a quick hop here over to Inchmahome. This is still a popular tourist island, with ferries running here in the summer months.

Once you have explored Inchmahome, don't miss Inch Talla and the castle remains. These are less commonly visited and you are likely to have this island all to yourself.

Back on the water, head south-west to a clearing on the shore. From here, it is possible to visit two sites of historic interest. One is the 'cup and ring marked stone' situated on the way to Loch Macanrie, a relic thought to date from the Bronze age, which is of historic and ritualistic importance. The other, to the south-east of Loch Macanrie is the site of the mysterious Black Loch Crannog, once a waterside residence and now a relic of an ancient and often forgotten loch.

Head north again on the western shores and follow the loch all the way round toward the jetty on the east and back toward the car park. Be aware of ferries coming to and from the jetty during the summer months.

Bonspiel

'Bonspiel' is an infrequent outdoor curling competition on the lake, which regularly freezes over in winter. Why not see how far you can curl a kayak?

15 River Teith

Get on / off	NN 624 079 / NN 668 044
Time required	3+ hours
Distance	4km or 10km
Parking / shuttle	NN 624 079 / NN 668 045 or NN 721 012
Water levels	0.5m +
Grade	1/2

Introduction

The Teith is a combination of two higher rivers, the Garbh Uisge (River Leny) and the Eas Gobhain, which flows from Loch Venachar. The Gaelic name for the river (Uisge Theamhich) translates as quiet and pleasant water.

This river has a special place with regard to the idiom 'armed to the teeth'. While it is heavily debated and only one of the many theories banded around, there is speculation that the saying comes from this river. Highland tribes would come down to sell their wool to those who lived in the lowlands once or twice every year and would always be

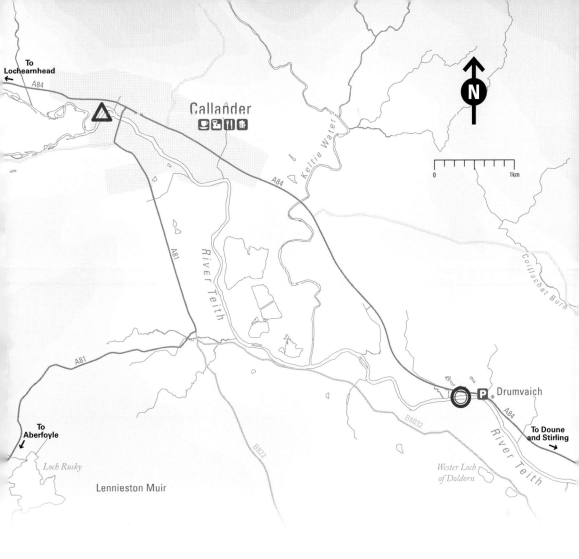

heavily armed. This caused tensions to run high and fights to break out. Needing a clear and defined boundary, the king chose the River Teith as the place they would leave their weapons on their way south; they would be 'armed to the teith'.

Brig O'Teith at Doune was built out of spite by Robert Spittall, tailor to the queen. He was refused passage in 1535, quite justifiably as he had no money. After taking the long way home, he returned to the area and built a bridge over the river, putting the ferryman out of work.

Callander, where this trip starts, is one of the more popular tourist towns in the Trossachs and there are a number of cafés, perfect for breakfast on your way to the river. Don't forget to pick up a pie from Mhor Bread for your lunch too.

Trip overview

Access from the main car park in Callander and be sure to pay for parking.

The river starts at the meadows in Callander, where the low flow and meandering nature makes for perfect access and warm up territory. So long as the river isn't in the car park here, you're good to go. If it's higher than this, the river is still often paddled, but becomes a very fast, much more dynamic environment, much less suitable for beginners or club paddlers.

A popular trip for clubs and beginners, as well as progressive and leadership courses, this can be a busy place. Don't be put off though, this long and winding river is perfect for everyone. Generally a gentle grade 1/2 river, this has some waves and playspots on which to hone your skills, or you can enjoy it as a gentle trip.

The route

If you want a warm up or a bit of practise before heading down river, paddle up to where the Leny ends and use the gentle flow here.

Immediately after the car park access you paddle under a magnificent red sandstone bridge and the river picks up speed as it leaves Callander behind. Shortly after here gentle rapids start to form and there are loads of opportunities to hit eddies and practise your skills, or just float down and enjoy the gentle gradient of the river.

The rapids are all grade 1/2 and can be run without inspection. Some bends have small holes and waves which can be surfed, or easily avoided if they're not your thing. Although this is a pleasant and relaxed river, some of the rapids still require active paddling to avoid being pushed into the outside of a bend, trees or rocks.

For the most part, the river banks are open fields with plenty of eddies and places to stop and regroup, stretch your legs or have lunch.

As you approach the end of the trip you reach the left hand bend of the Torrie rapid. This usually runs cleanly down a chute on river left, but can be rocky at lower water levels.

The egress point is about 800 metres below Torrie, on river left. Climb out on the bank and follow the track to the A84 and take care when crossing the road to the lay-by.

16 The Black Water

Get on / off	NN 508 069 / NN 560 062
Time required	1–3 hours
Distance	7km
Parking / shuttle	NN 509 070 / NN 560 062
Water levels	0.5m +

Introduction

This narrow, tree-lined river is a true woodland adventure, linking Loch Achray and Loch Venachar. Once part of the waterworks for Glasgow's drinking water, this river is now quite overgrown. The lower reaches are lined with farmland and it's not uncommon to see sheep and the occasional cow down by the river for a drink.

The Byre Inn offers accommodation as well as food and drinks and an almost constant playlist of happy hardcore.

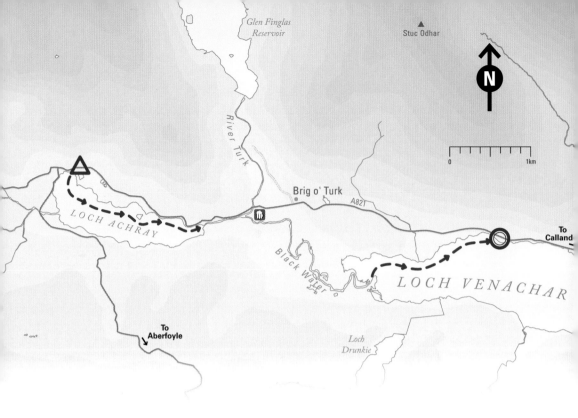

Trip overview

Parking is easiest at the west end of Loch Achray, and this trip is most commonly combined with the parking on Loch Achray and Loch Venachar.

Overhanging trees and some tight bends on the river make general boat handling a necessary skill. Watch out also for blockages and be ready to pull into the side and portage some sections. At low flows these aren't an issue, but the river can become quite fast after heavy rain.

The route

The hardest thing about this river is often finding the start. At the east end of Loch Achray is a small thicket of trees. Aim straight at these and the start of a river will materialise slowly in front of you.

Generally you can follow this river with minimal concerns, but be on your toes and keep an eye on what is ahead; be aware of the possibility of fallen trees and river-wide blockages. There are a few small rapids on this river, some of which can be quite shallow. Others have a tendency to push the unwary towards overhanging trees, especially after heavy rains.

The river opens up for the final 500 metres and meanders its way onto Loch Venachar. The closest car park here is on the northern shore almost directly across the loch.

Breaking ice on Loch Dochart \ Photo Paddlemore

Breadalbane

A large historic province within Scotland, Breadalbane (Bràghad Albann) itself covers a much wider geographical area than that which sits within the park. Prior to the 1400s, Breadalbane was part of Athol, but the area now known as Breadalbane was awarded to Colin Campbell by King James II as a reward for his capture of the assassins of King James I. The parliamentary title given to the area, 'Earl of Breadalbane' is historically bestowed upon a member of the Campbell family.

The area within the park extends down as far as Callander and over to Killin, another popular tourist town. This section contains much of the watershed of the Tay network which flows out eventually into the sea at Dundee and is, by capacity, Scotland's largest river.

Away from the water, this section contains the largest munro in the park – Ben Mor, and Crianlarich, once the most popular crossroads in Scotland. This small town is now largely forgotten since the building of a bypass to speed up transport links to the highlands.

There are six lochs and four rivers in this area. Similarly to the Trossachs, these are often overlooked in favour of the larger and better-known Loch Lomond, but the history and beauty in this area often means that once you've paddled in Breadalbane, you will keep returning.

OPEN WATER

17 Loch Doine and Voil

18 Loch Lubnaig

19 Loch Earn

20 Loch Dochart and Iubhair

RIVERS

21 River Dochart – Easy WW Grade: 1–2 (2+/3)

21a Lix Toll and the Falls of Dochart – WW Grade: 3/4

22 River Leny – WW Grade: 3+/4 (5)

23 River Balvaig

A moody sky on Loch Voil \ Photo Paddlemore

17 Lochs Doine and Voil

Get on / off	NN 443 182 / NN 535 206
Time required	1–3 hours
Distance	7.5km
Parking / shuttle	NN 443 182 / NN 535 206

Introduction

At the end of the road up Balquhidder Glen is the small village of Inverlochlarig, where Rob Roy Macgregor died in December 1734. His home once stood where the farm is now located and he was buried in the graveyard at Balquhidder Church at the east end of Loch Voil. The road to the north of the lochs which links these two places is often referred to as the 'coffin road'; the famous outlaw and folk hero was carried along here from his death bed to his final resting place.

On Loch Voil you will see the northern shore littered with many large historic homes. One of these, Monachyle Mhor, now operates as a top end hotel which could make this a very comfortable overnight adventure.

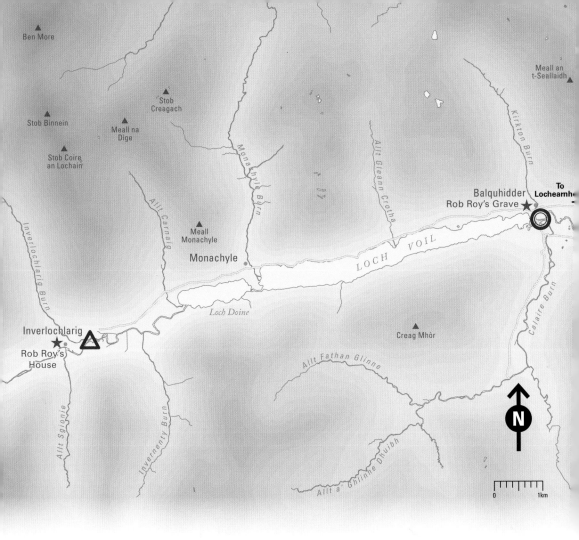

The southern shore, meanwhile, is wooded with many secluded spots which are perfect for a quiet overnight bivi or camp spot.

Trip overview

This trip starts on the River Larig. It is best to park at the Inverlochlarig walker's car park and walk the short distance to the ford where access is possible.

We have linked the two lochs together as a linear, one-way trip, but you could make it most of the way back to Loch Doine, although you would have to walk the final couple of kilometres to the car park unless you fancy yourself as an upstream expert. Alternatively if you wish to make the route circular, park at the east end of Loch Voil (marked as the get-out for this route) and paddle up and back from here.

Loch Doine is only a couple of kilometres long, with Loch Voil being the bulk of the trip. These lochs are narrow and sheltered, rarely being too wind affected to paddle. Standing at the eastern end of Loch Voil and looking out over the water, you could be almost anywhere in the highlands. Rugged mountains line the loch and it appears to go on endlessly.

The route

For the first kilometre or so of the trip you are carried by the gentle flow of the River Larig. Before long you emerge onto Loch Doine and head eastward, generally along the southern shore toward the narrows and then Loch Voil.

The loch is 5.5km long and becomes narrower as you head eastward. Again, we recommend the southern shore of the loch simply to avoid being right next to the road. This said, the loch is only a few hundred metres wide and is a good place to spend some time away from the shore. Weather and skill permitting, a paddle down the middle of this loch gives you some incredible views.

Eventually you will arrive at the village of Balquhidder, where you can egress by the bridge over the River Balvaig, or follow the river downstream towards Loch Lubnaig (see next trip).

© Loch Lubnaig | Photo PaddleMore

18 Loch Lubnaig

Get on / off	NN 586 107
Time required	3+ hours
Distance	14km
Parking / shuttle	NN 586 107

Introduction

The loch takes its name from a prominent bend about halfway along, and the name itself translates as "crooked loch". The loch narrows at the crook and can almost feel like two distinct bodies of water.

The Rob Roy Way lines the eastern shore, doubling as a National Cycle Network trail. It follows in the footsteps of that famous Scottish outlaw; Breadalbane is truly his country. He was born and lived out most of his life in the area, and now resides just up the road in Balquhidder cemetery. These tracks were also regularly used during the Jacobite rebellions, an uprising against English monarchic rule in Scotland.

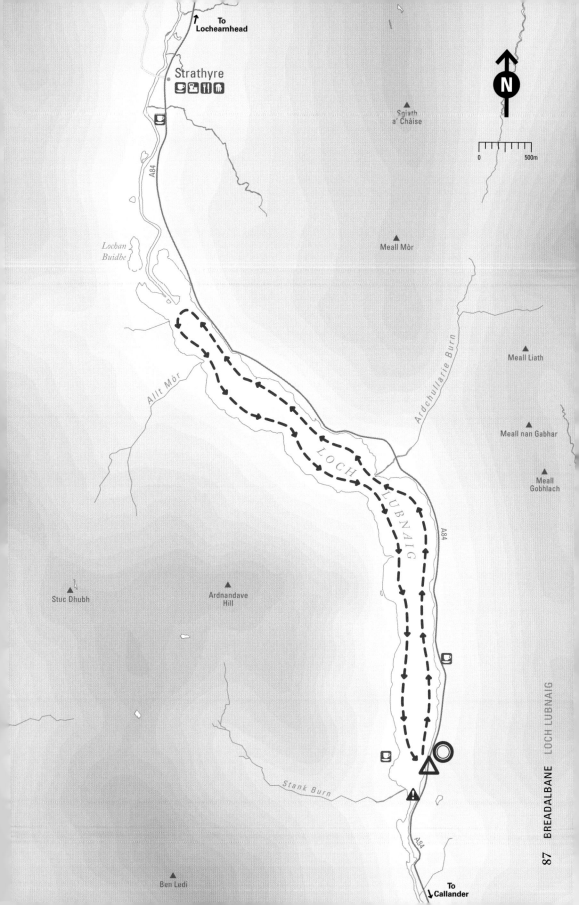

To
Lochearnhead

Strathyre

A84

Lochan
Buidhe

Allt Mòr

Sgiath
a' Chàise

Meall Mòr

Meall Liath

Meall nan Gabhar

Meall
Gobhlach

LOCH LUBNAIG

A84

Ardchullarie Burn

Stuc Dhubh

Ardnandave
Hill

Stank Burn

Ben Ledi

To
Callander

A84

N

0   500m

At the southern end of the loch is the submerged site of a crannog. During particularly warm summers, when the level of the loch drops significantly, you can sometimes see the stilts which once supported the building protruding from the water.

Trip overview

From the get-on you can decide whether to explore clockwise or anti-clockwise, usually depending on the prevailing wind.

The crook from which the loch takes its name can be found as it narrows at Ardchullarie Burn. Also, to the north, there are two hidden features of this loch. In particularly wet weather the marshes flood and you can access Lochan Buidhe. During prolonged spells of this wet weather, Loch Lubnaig and Voil can both flood, turning the end of the River Balvaig into Loch Occasional!

The route

Head north toward the crook and narrows. Follow the eastern shores here and paddle north until you reach the head of the loch. You can explore the end of the River Balvaig here and the wetlands surrounding it before following the Rob Roy Way south, down the western shore. This is the more interesting shoreline and some people choose to follow this in both directions so as to be away from the busy road on the eastern shore. There are many spurs and bays as you head south, as well as points to stop and explore on foot.

As you reach the southern end, look out for the crannog. The River Leny leaves to the south, and the top reaches of this river are slow, enclosed and beautiful. Many people will choose to delve into them before paddling back upstream. Be aware of your surroundings, however, and turn back before the river narrows and picks up speed, there is some serious white water downstream. This is also a common place to practise upstream skills.

Birds of Prey

The mountains surrounding the loch are home to many species of birds of prey and they are often seen soaring over the loch as they hunt.

19 Loch Earn

Get on / off	NN 593 237
Time required	3+ hours
Distance	14km
Parking / shuttle	NN 592 238

Introduction

The 10km long Loch Earn, known as "the loch of the Irish", was the historic boundary between Pictland and Dalriada (Dál Riata), the kingdom of the Scots who came from Ireland – Dundurn at the east end of the loch being a Pictish frontier fort. This supports the belief that the word Earn came from the Gaelic, Eireann.

As with much of the park the loch and its surrounding area is steeped in historical interest; at the Lochearnhead end of the loch there are two buildings of note. Edinample Castle was built as home to 'Black' Duncan Campbell of Glenorchy in 1630; Ardvorlich House was the home of the Stewarts of Ardvorlich since 1580, and was the final resting place of the seven Macdonalds of Glencoe killed while attempting a raid on Ardvorlich House in 1620.

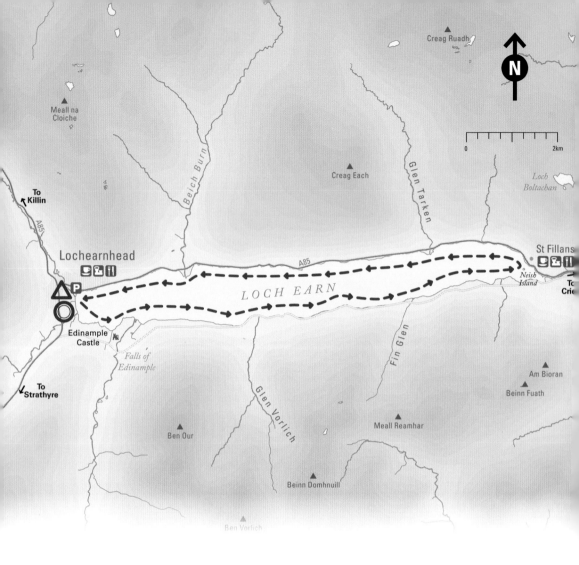

Just onto the water from Edinample, if you look beneath you, you'll see the remains of an old crannog. In the planning stages of the Crannog Centre on Loch Tay this submerged artifact was researched closely to ensure accuracy of the new building.

Also on the southern shore, a memorial stone marks the place of the temporary interment of Major James Stewart, who died in 1662. Although reasons for his initial burial here vary, one story suggests that the McNabs were threatening to intercept the funeral procession, which was headed for St Fillans, and so rather than risk a fight, they buried the Major near Ardvorlich before moving him at a later date.

Meanwhile down toward St Fillans, the small island just offshore has a colourful history. Originally man-made for a Pictish crannog site, it was then the site of a castle built by the Neish clan in the 13th century. Twelve members of the McNab clan, of Killin, surprised the inhabitants with a night time raid, having carried a boat over the hills from Loch

Tay. They overran the castle, of which nothing now remains, but grew tired of carrying the boat home. They left the boat on the hillside where it remained for hundreds of years, eventually being destroyed in a peat fire.

Trip overview

There are a number of places to access the loch. There are six large laybys along the northern road (A85), many of which are also informal campsites, and you can also access at St Fillans.

We have chosen to start our route from Lochearnhead. Here there is a large public car park, and facilities (summer only) and it's just a short crossing to launch on the beach.

The loch is narrow and runs east to west, sheltered from the north and south by sizable mountains. The wind can be wild on Loch Earn and the fetch is long enough to build sizeable waves in Lochearnhead or St Fillans.

The River Earn leaves the loch in St Fillans and while it is not in the park, it is a commonly paddled river; although generally people start further downstream as the top section is overgrown and heavily wooded.

The route

Cross the loch to Edinample and explore the site of the crannog. From here, head east following the southern shore. You'll soon reach Ardvorlich House, the start of the route up Ben Vorlich. This is a good option for a combined walking and paddling trip, but the area sees a lot of traffic, so we recommend securing your kit before heading off into the hills. Just along from here is the memorial stone to Major James Stewart, then a further 5km will bring you to the Loch Earn Leisure Park at Ardtrostan before you arrive at St Fillans.

The village of St Fillans is a great spot to stop for lunch, with a number of small cafés and hotels. As you leave St Fillans following the northern shore be sure to keep an eye out for fishing lines from the many who utilise this bank.

If you are looking for a multi-day adventure you can stop at Woodhouse and wander up Glen Tarken to take in the fantastic views.

20 Lochs Dochart and Iubhair

Get on / off	NN 410 258 / NN 425 267
Time required	1–3 hours
Distance	5km
Parking / shuttle	NN 410 258 / NN 425 267

Introduction

These lochs are often overlooked, driven by in pursuit of alternative adventure, or otherwise used to access the River Dochart (see next description). However, they are very accessible, and rich in terms of historical interest.

Loch Dochart itself has a range of channels and a few small islands, one of which contains Dochart Castle, dating back as far as the fifteen hundreds. This castle was built on the site of an old religious building, most likely linked with St Fillans Priory just upriver from here. These waterways were a major link in the pre-industrial age, allowing transport of goods from the highlands, down the Tay network and out to the Forth of Firth.

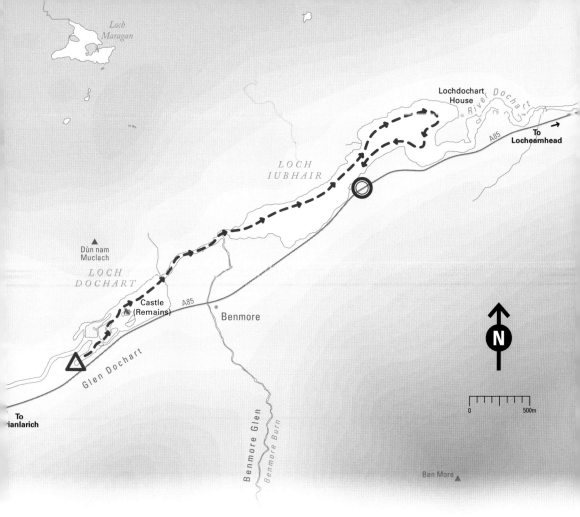

Loch Iubhair, commonly misspelled, is pronounced yoo-ar and means yew loch. This beautiful loch meanders its way to become the upper reaches of the River Dochart. Many of the spurs are separated by just a small walkway from the mainland, and take on the appearance of small islands. On most of these you will find local farm animals making the most of the abundance of plant life down by the water.

Trip overview

Park at the east end of Loch Dochart and access from here. The parking is relatively limited, so it's recommended to leave more vehicles at Loch Iubhair.

These two lochs can be explored individually, or alternatively, a short linear route can connect the two bodies of water together. This is an easy shuttle and simply requires parking further along the A85 wherever you decide you would like to egress.

The narrows down to Loch Iubhair have a gentle flow, and could be navigated upstream to make this a circular route, so long as you have the appropriate upstream traditional paddling / poling skills. Alternatively this is a good place to practise them.

The route

Once on the water, follow the southern shore of Loch Dochart to where the loch becomes fragmented. These sections can be explored, but are very dependent on water levels as to how deep they are. On your way back down the northern shore, stop at the island in the middle and explore the remains of Dochart Castle. The castle is a pretty cool camping spot, especially for younger children.

Join the narrow passage in the north east of the loch, and allow the gentle flow to carry you down to loch Iubhair.

Here, follow the northern shore along the Lochdochart House at the east end, and explore the upper section of the River Dochart, without being swept downstream. The first couple of bends of the river are wide and mellow and you can usually get back upstream. If you find yourself going too far, get off by the first bridge and carefully make your way back to your vehicle.

Follow the southern shore back up and get off roughly halfway along the loch at the picnic site and car park.

This trip can be combined with the touring section of the River Dochart to make for a long day or a relaxed overnight trip.

21 River Dochart

Get on / off	NN 425 267 / NN 504 286
Time required	1–3 hours
Distance	10km
Parking / shuttle	NN 425 267 / NN 504 286
Optimum water level	0.75+
Grade	1–2 (2+/3)

Introduction

The Dochart is the primary inflow for Loch Tay. The river ends just outside the park boundary and is a real mixed bag containing everything from gentle green flow to serious white water.

The Falls of Dochart, in Killin, is a major tourist attraction and the bridge over it can become almost impassable in the summer months. On the island just to the right of the river, after the bridge, are the burial grounds for clan McNab, one of the most historically important families in the area. In 1646 John McNab burnt down Dochart Castle, up on Loch Dochart, after a long-running political feud with the Campbells who had built it.

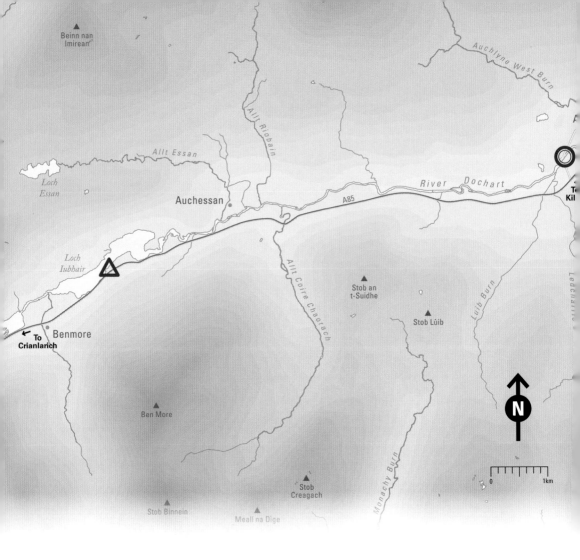

Also in Killin is Fingal's stone, memorial and burial place of the legendary giant of Scottish folklore. There are a number of cafés and shops in Killin, and the Falls of Dochart Inn overlooks the river on the edge of town.

Trip overview

The section from Loch Iubhair to Auchlyne Bridge is a fantastic touring section with sections of grade 1 and 2 with one larger, easy to portage grade 2+ (grade 3 in high water).

The route

Leaving Loch Iubhair, the River Dochart meanders down to the first grade 2 rapid under the bridge at Auchessan, where a number of good small surf waves form. The river continues through the beautiful glen, often following the old military road or old rail line. A number of short grade 2 rapids break up the straightforward grade 1 which precede the larger grade (2+/3). This larger rapid is easily spotted as a horizon line is obvious from 100m upstream; inspection / portage can be easily managed on river right. From here the river flows down grade 1 sections to the Auchlyne Bridge where the get-out is on river left.

21A LIX TOLL AND THE FALLS OF DOCHART

Grade 3/4

For those looking to do a more extreme trip, the Lix Toll to Loch Tay section (best accessed from NN 548 309 on the back road between Auchlyne Bridge and the village of Killin) is a more challenging grade 3 with the long, impressive, grade 4 Falls of Dochart.

The rapids at Lix Toll are tight, technical and contain many hidden holes (grade 3). The river continues to build and enters the small village of Killin, passing the War Memorial on river right. There is access here where inspection of the Falls of Dochart is both possible and recommended.

The Falls of Dochart is an 800m long grade 4 rapid with a river wide stopper forming under the bridge, so inspection is highly recommended. There is a small pool just after the bridge at most levels, but this is short lived before another series of ledge style rapids which can form some serious holes. There is a get-out 300m downstream on river right at the old railway bridge, which is a bit of a scramble out. Alternatively, you can paddle all the way down to Loch Tay and back up the River Lochy to the Killin Hotel NN 572 332.

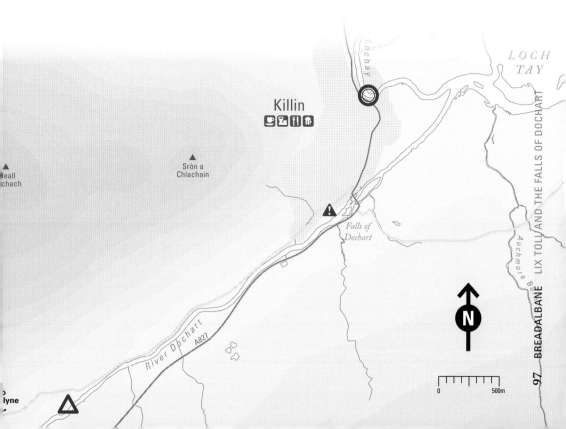

22 River Leny

Get on / off	NN 586 095 / NN 608 082
Time required	1–3 hours for a first run, can be paddle in 30 minutes.
Distance	3km
Parking / shuttle	NN 586 095 / NN 608 082
Optimum water level	0.75+
Grade	3+/4 (5)

Introduction

The River Leny isn't the true name for the river. Its true, Gaelic name is Garbh Uisge, which translates as Rough Water in English. The name of Leny comes from the Pass of Leny, which runs from the Leny House and Estate in Glen Leny to Loch Lubnaig and the rest of Breadalbane. The pass gives its name to the falls on the Garbh Uisge but not the river. The Leny Burn can be found flowing through Glen Leny, which runs north / south and lies between the village of Kilmahog and the town of Callander.

The National Cycle Network route 7 follows this river, making it straightforward to shuttle with just one vehicle.

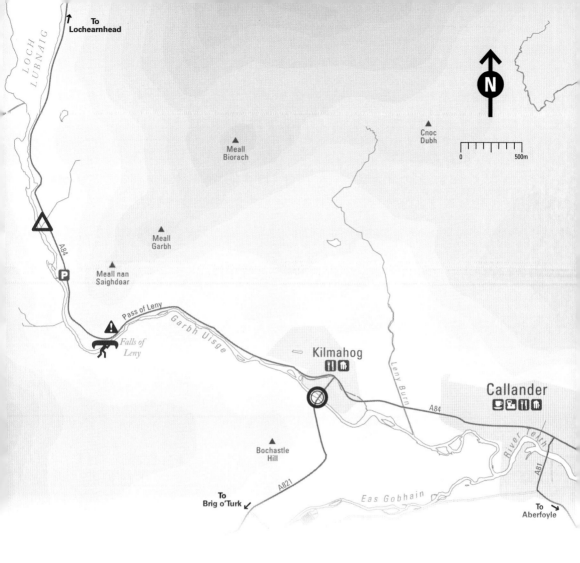

Trip overview

Parking is possible either in a long layby off the A84, or in the Ben Ledi car park. This car park fills up quickly with walkers on weekends and during the summer. We tend to stick to the layby if we have a shuttle vehicle, but the Ben Ledi car park is perfect for a single vehicle run, and avoids a stretch of walking alongside the main road.

This short 3km section of grade 3/4 broken up with the Falls of Leny (grade 5) is one of the Scottish white-water classics. With the river being fed from Loch Lubnaig, it takes considerable rain to bring it into condition but generally remains paddleable for several days following heavy rainfall.

Be aware that this river is often used for safety and rescue courses by various paddle sport providers and the fire service.

The route

Starting on a wide gentle section flowing out of Loch Lubnaig, the river winds down under a bridge and things start to steepen up. A long grade 3 rapid with lots of fun waves, small holes and eddies, leads you down to just above the Falls of Leny (grade 5). A large eddy on river right allows inspection and portage, don't forget about the exit drop (grade 4) that is easily missed on inspection.

Below the Falls and exit drop, there is a large pool perfect for regrouping before heading down through Wee Stinker and S Bends, both grade 3/4 with some meaty holes at higher water levels (inspection / portage river right).

After S Bends the river calms to grade 2/3 and carries you down to the get-out at Kilmahog car park immediately after the stone bridge. The eddy here isn't always great and you often just have to beach yourself and hold on to the bank to avoid washing downstream.

23 River Balvaig

Get on / off	NN 535 206 / NN 559 168
Time required	1–3 hours
Distance	3km
Parking / shuttle	NN 535 206 / NN 560 168
Optimum water level	Almost always flows.
Grade	1

Introduction

The Balvaig drains Loch Voil and links it to Loch Lubnaig. Although this meandering river runs through farmland, the high banks on either side give you a feeling of seclusion and shelter.

The forestry commission car park at the get-out is the old site of the Dun Lubnaig Broch, an Iron Age drystone hollow-walled structure which was rebuilt between 2004–2007. Also in this car park is The Broch Café, which we recommend stopping at before or after the river. Or both.

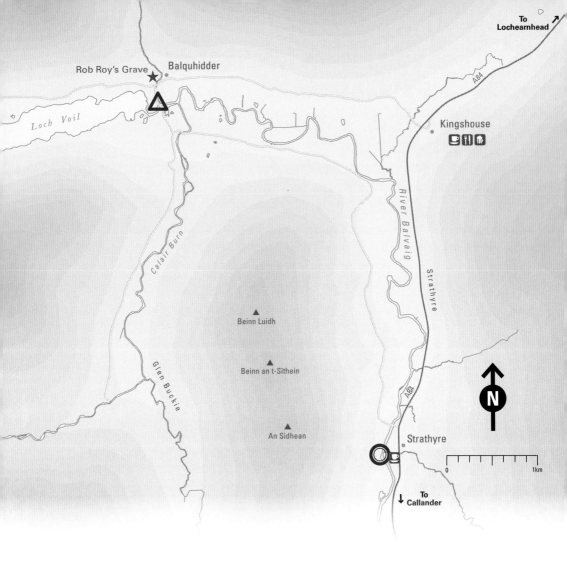

If you follow this river all the way to Loch Lubnaig, you are likely to see oystercatchers, among other wading birds, who flock to the wetlands after heavy rain to take advantage of the enormous amount of food on offer. After prolonged periods of heavy rain, this section can flood and becomes known as 'Loch Occasional'.

Trip overview

To access from Loch Voil, you park right at the stone bridge where the river leaves the loch. It's usually easiest to get on just below this bridge, and the first few rapids can be shallow and shingley. This is a great beginners' river, with gentle white water linked together by flat sections of flow.

The National Cycle Network route 7 follows this river, making it straightforward to shuttle with just one vehicle.

The route

The river can often be shallow until the Calair Burn joins on river right 100m downstream of the bridge. The Calair burn joins shortly downstream and from here the river meanders through rich farmland with small shingle rapids following the main flow of the river.

The river turns and starts to flow south towards Loch Lubnaig shortly after passing Stroneslaney House, one of the only buildings at the river's edge. Be careful as there are often cables crossing the river here, usually above head height, which are part of a system to haul goods across the river.

A further 3km and an old stone bridge marks your entrance into the village of Strathyre. As the river flows through the village it deepens and is a great place to practise your rescue skills before finishing the trip on the large beach on river left upstream of the regenerated bridge.

Loch Goil from Carrick Castle \ Photo PaddleMore

Cowal

When the Irish invaded the region we now know as Cowal (Comhghall), it became part of their Kingdom of Dal Riata. Control of the area was given to the Cenél Comgall from who we get the Gaelic name Comgaill.

This area of the park is often overlooked, which is strange as it is one of the most beautiful. With the stunning Benmore Botanic Gardens and the Argyll Forest Park, Cowal's plant life is second to none. This section covers the lochs and rivers of this hidden gem, along with the three sea lochs that lie on the boundary of the park.

OPEN WATER

24 Loch Eck

25 Holy Loch

26 Loch Long

27 Loch Goil

RIVERS

28 River Eachaig – Easy WW Grade 1–2

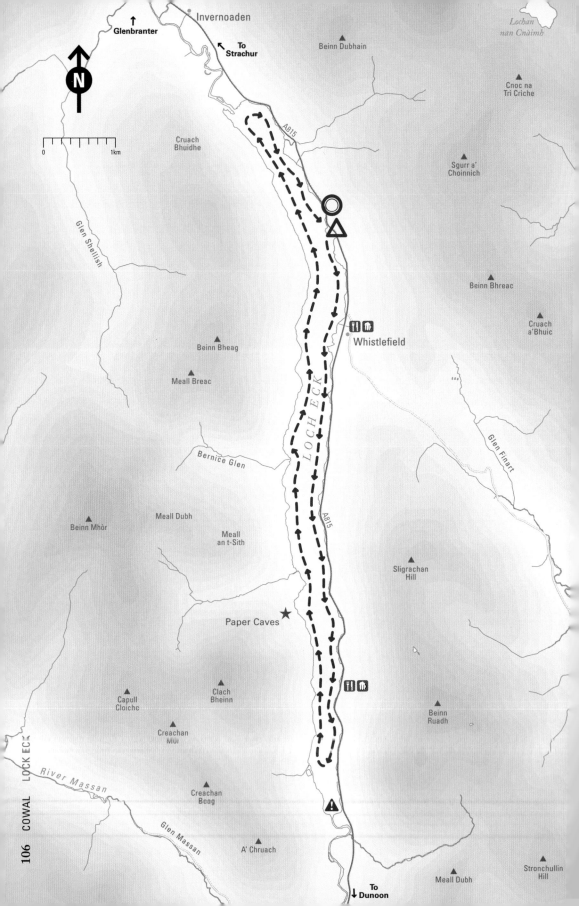

Inveroaden

Glenbranter

To
Strachur

N

0   1km

Lochan
nan Cnùimh

Beinn Dubhain

Cnoc na
Trì Criche

A815

Sgurr a'
Choinnich

Cruach
Bhuidhe

Beinn Bhreac

Cruach
a'Bhuic

Whistlefield

LOCH ECK

Beinn Bheag

Meall Breac

Bernice Glen

Glen Shellish

Meall Dubh

Beinn Mhòr

Meall
an t-Sith

A815

Sligrachan
Hill

Glen Finart

Paper Caves

Capull
Cloiche

Clach
Bheinn

Beinn
Ruadh

Creachan
Mòr

Creachan
Beag

River Massan

A' Chruach

Glen Massan

Meall Dubh

Stronchullin
Hill

To
Dunoon

24 Loch Eck

Get on / off	NS 141 946
Time required	1–3 hours
Distance	18km
Parking / shuttle	NS 141 946

Introduction

At the base of Beinn Mhor sits the 11 kilometres of Loch Eck (Loch Eich). There are many wild camping spots along the shores with peninsulas and bays combining for an interesting, relaxing adventure.

The loch is famous for the Paper Caves (NS 136 894), which are a short walk through the woods on the western shore. These caves take their name from the story about the 9th Earl of Argyll, who is believed to have hidden his family land deeds in these caves, securing their right to the land, were it ever to be captured by his enemies.

At the head of the loch, at Invernoaden, is the Lauder Memorial. Erected in 1921 by Sir Harry Lauder, this memorial pays homage to his son John who was killed in France in World War I. John was to inherit the land as an engagement gift.

Trip overview

You'll be able to easily access the loch on its eastern shore from many of the car parks and laybys along the A815, or alternatively, at the Forestry Commission offices and car park at Glenbranter at the northern end of the loch. The latter gives you a two kilometre section of winding jungle adventure burn to take you to the loch itself.

Although the loch is narrow, on average just 500m, don't get lulled into a false sense of security; it can still bring plenty of challenges in windy conditions.

About halfway down the eastern shore you pass Whistlefield, where a popular pub / restaurant of the same name can offer a welcome break. Further down this shore is the Coylet Inn, accessible almost directly from the water, which would serve as a perfect halfway lunch stop.

Take care at the most southerly point where the River Eachaig leaves the loch. The man-made weir here is best avoided. For those choosing to carry on down the river (see 28 River Eachaig, page 120), portaging is usually preferable and can be easily managed on the river right.

The route

Follow the eastern shore southwards using the many peninsulas and picnic spots to stop if necessary. Head past Whistlefield and the Coylet Inn further down, and take care to stay upstream of the weir at the southern end, as you pass the outflow of the Eachaig.

Turn back north and follow the western shore back to the top of the loch. This western shore has plenty of bays and peninsulas, perfect for an overnight camp; just watch out for the cows which run wild here! Access the paper caves roughly a third of the way up this shore.

Powan fish

The Powan fish have inhabited Scotland's lochs since the last ice age. They were trapped by the receding ice and made their homes in the water which was left. Nowadays they're threatened almost to extinction, their eggs being a favoured food of the invasive and rapid-breeding Ruffe.

Loch Eck is one of just two waterways these fish now naturally occur in, the other being Loch Lomond. Keep an eye out for their distinctive dark blueish, or green backs swimming underneath your boats.

© Holy Loch / Ifan Drafael Taylor

25 Holy Loch

Get on / off	NS 162 804 / NS 191 884
Time required	1–3 hours
Distance	10km
Parking / shuttle	NS 162 804 / NS 191 884

This is a sea loch, but other than the taste, the only real difference is that sometimes you have to walk a bit further from your car. There are no real tidal stream considerations, but the weather off the Clyde can get pretty wild sometimes.

Introduction

Despite its small size the Holy Loch (An Loch Sianta / Seunta) has a rich history. The original Gaelic name for the loch, 'An Loch Seunta', meaning 'the enchanted / spellbound

LOCH ECK

A815

Sligrachan
Hill

Castle
Crag

Glen Finart Burn

Stronvochlan

Shepherd's Point

Beinn
Ruadh

Ardentinny

Coulport

Meall Dubh

Stronchullin
Hill

LOCH LONG

Ardpeaton

Stronchullin Burn

River Eachaig

Creag Mhòr

Gairletter Point

Blairmore
Hill

A815

Ardbeg

Kilmun
Hill

A880

Blairmore

Sandhaven

A815

HOLY LOCH

Kilmun

Graham's
Point

Strone

Gibb's
Point

Strone Point

Sandbank

Lazaretto
Point

Ardnadam

A885

A815

Dunoon

N

0

loch' became 'An Loch Sianta' over time; this means 'the charmed or holy loch'. This is attributed to Saint Munn who was an early patron of Christianity, significant here in spreading the religion in the area.

Fintán of Taghmon, as he was known in Ireland, landed here from Ireland in the 6th century and formed his church at Kilmun. By the 15th century the significance of Kilmun as a local centre of Christianity was so great that the loch's name had changed.

By the turn of the 20th century the loch had changed significantly. With the arrival of ship building at the tail end of the 19th century, the loch was home to the famous yacht builders Alexander Robertson & Sons who built racing yachts, many of which still sail today. With the world wars starting, however, the loch changed once again and was part of the naval stronghold of HMNB (Her Majesty's Naval Base) Clyde. Throughout the war the loch was home to much of the British Atlantic Submarine Fleet, as well as hosting many US Naval ships for servicing and repairs. Both of these sites are now combined as the Holy Loch Marina.

The Americans then remained in and around the Holy Loch until 1992. The loch was home to the US Navy's Submarine Squadron 14, part of Submarine Force, U.S. Atlantic Fleet and Fleet Ballistic Missile Refit Site One.

Winds can funnel in from the sea and large waves can form at times. There is a long fetch due to the large distances here, and large waves form in relatively minor winds.

Trip overview

There are a number of places where you can access the loch, including the Holy Loch Marina. If you intend to launch at the marina it's best to contact them before pitching up and getting on the water. Alternatively you can access the bottom of the River Eachaig at the Cot House Garage, although parking here is limited.

This trip takes you round to Shepherd's Point, in Ardentinny, the finishing point for the Loch Long route, but you could go out and back comfortably in a day.

The route

Leave the marina and head along the south shore to Lazaretto Point. From here there is a short crossing to Graham's Point, on the northern shore. Follow this along until you reach the end of the Holy Loch.

Be very aware of weather conditions before leaving Gibb's Point, just further along from Graham's Point. Shortly after Gibb's Point, the beach gives way to a high Victorian sea wall and there is no escape point until you round the bend. The wind here comes straight off the Clyde and can push against rocks and the wall here with incredible ferocity.

Once you round the bend onto Loch Long, head north along the western shores until you pass the Gairletter Point Caravan Park, and then it's just three more kilometres until you reach Shepherd's Point.

Kilmun Church – Saint Munn

On the northern shores of the Holy Loch is Kilmun Church, where St Munn based his 7th century monastic community. The remains of a 12th century church can still be seen, but much of the modern building was finished in the 19th century.

This is an epicentre of Scottish Christianity, and also home to a Clan Campbell mausoleum, originating in the 17th century when the family held nearby Dunoon Castle.

26 Loch Long

Get on / off	NN 295 049 / NS 191 884
Time required	3+ hours
Distance	40km / 20km
Parking / shuttle	NN 295 049 / NS 191 884

This is a sea loch, but other than the taste, the only real difference is that sometimes you have to walk a bit further from your car. There are no real tidal considerations, but the weather off the Clyde can get pretty wild sometimes.

Introduction

This 32km long sea loch has a rich and varied history, from viking pillagers to modern day military establishments. The Finnart Oil Terminal and Coulport military base dominate the eastern shore, but the west is a trove of coves and peninsulas to explore. Wildlife lives here in abundance, with seals, porpoise and the occasional pilot whale coming inland to explore the loch.

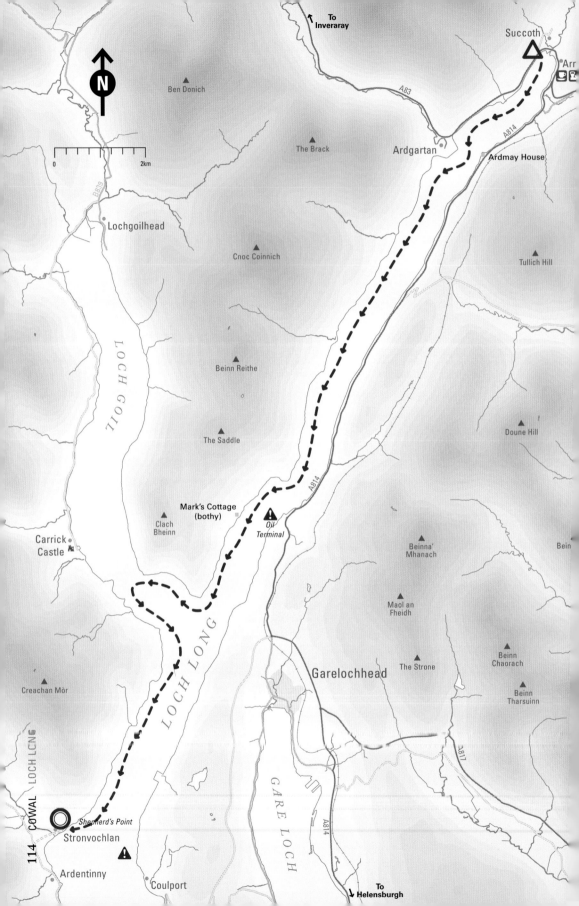

Wrecks

Divers, the rubber clad type, frequent the loch floor up near Arrochar, at the head of the loch. The many wrecks which are there are of continued interest to that community, but they do have to be careful of the conger eels which call the loch bed home.

As the name suggests, it's a long piece of water, but it's also ridiculously straight for such a long loch. Because of this, the military previously used Loch Long as a torpedo testing range, and the control hub for this was on the western shore roughly opposite modern day Ardmay House. The old jetty and abandoned building are still there today.

Winds can funnel in from the sea and large waves can form in relatively minor winds.

Trip overview

Starting from Arrochar it's possible to do a number of trips depending on how much of a time you have and what craft you want to play with. The loch stretches all the way to the Holy Loch and the Firth of Clyde meaning there's loads to explore; however parts of the eastern shore are military zones which must be avoided, unless you're keen to spend some time in handcuffs.

The car park at Succoth, just past Arrochar, sits at the head of the loch and allows easy access. Arrochar itself has a handful of shops and takeaways to stock up from and buy breakfast as you start your journey. This loch is commonly linked with other areas, but can also be explored as a stand-alone venue as a linear or 'there and back again' route.

The route

We recommend leaving Arrochar and following the western shore south. The eastern shore follows the road, and has both Finnart Oil Terminal, where they refill tankers, and further south a militarised zone into which access is forbidden. These issues, and the fact that the western shore is considerably more interesting and scenic, lead us to the unusual recommendation that you do not make this a circular trip, but rather head out and back along the western shore.

Soon after leaving Arrochar you pass Ardgartan Hotel, an impressive building full of coach tourists, and, on the opposite shore, Ardmay House, an outdoor centre. In the summer you may see youngsters from the centre out on the water.

Head south past Coillessan, a small collection of buildings down by the water, and after another six kilometres you will come to Mark's Cottage, opposite Finnart.

Mark's Cottage is a bothy which sits roughly two kilometres before the junction with Loch Goil. This is an idyllic overnight spot. It is important that bothy users follow the code and guidelines set down by the Mountain Bothy Association. This is also an appropriate spot to have lunch and turn back if you don't fancy the lengthy crossing over the mouth of Loch Goil.

The mouth of Loch Goil measures at just over a kilometre and in more difficult conditions it may be advisable to enter the loch a short way before crossing. Beyond this point the trip continues in a similar fashion and has some excellent areas to explore. Four kilometres after crossing Loch Goil, you will reach Shepherd's Point, down near Stronvochlan. This is where we end the trip and recommend turning back toward Arrochar. Alternatively, this is an option for an egress if you want a linear trip, or camping if you want to make this an overnight experience. Beyond here, the road rejoins Loch Long and the waterway becomes quite committing, taking you down to the Firth of Clyde, a tidal estuary with wild and unpredictable weather.

The military zone on the eastern shore has a 'no access' area on the water which is enforced by police boats.

27 Loch Goil

Get on / off	NN 199 012
Time required	3+ hours
Distance	15km
Parking / shuttle	NN 199 012

This is a sea loch, but other than the taste, the only real difference is that sometimes you have to walk a bit further from your car. There are no real tidal considerations, but the weather off the Clyde can get pretty wild sometimes.

Introduction

Linking Loch Long to the village of Lochgoilhead, this inland sea loch plays host to an array of wildlife seldom seen throughout other areas of the park. Pods of porpoise, diving shags and harem of seals are likely to join you as you paddle down the loch.

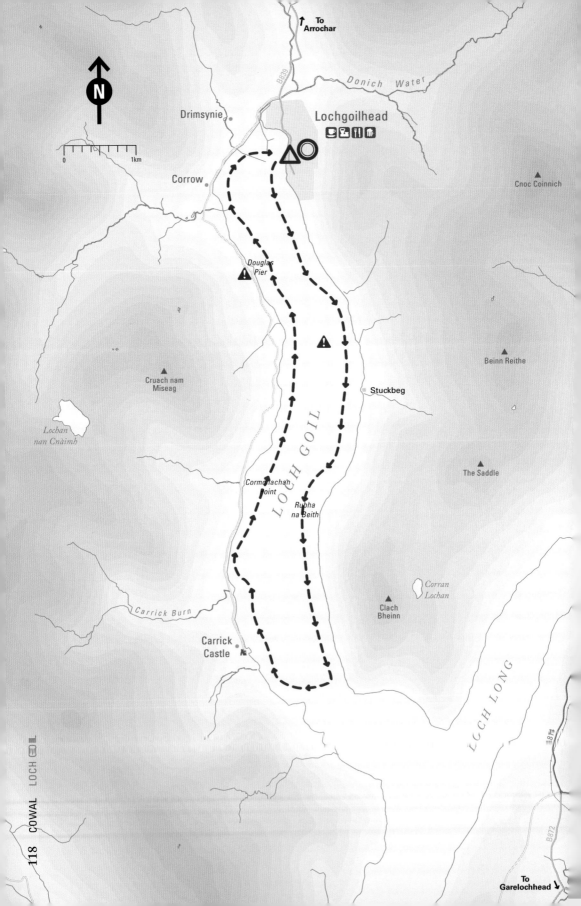

COWAL LOCH

To Arrochar

Donich Water

Drimsynie

Lochgoilhead

Cnoc Coinnich

Corrow

Douglas Pier

Beinn Reithe

Cruach nam Miseag

Stuckbeg

Lochan nan Cnàimh

LOCH GOIL

The Saddle

Cormonachan Point

Rubha na Beith

Corran Lochan

Clach Bheinn

LOCH LONG

Carrick Burn

Carrick Castle

N

0   1km

To Garelochhead

Carrick Castle, at the mouth of the loch, was an important outpost for Clan Campbell throughout the fifteen and sixteen hundreds. Mary Queen of Scots even visited back in 1563. It was later destroyed, bombarded by HMS Kingfisher during uprisings, and the remains were looted before being burnt. It was never fully restored, although nowadays scaffolding surrounds the building thanks to a dispute over permission to complete a secretly started building project.

Two prominent structures, Maytime and Mini Maytime, demonstrate the loch's ongoing military importance. Submarines from Faslane regularly come into the loch for routine maintenance and sonar testing. In this instance, the loch becomes a hive of activity, with police boats and military ribs, with mounted weapons buzzing around it.

Trip overview

This trip is commonly accessed from the village of Lochgoilhead, located several miles from the A83 from the Rest and Be Thankful. A small shop in the village allows for last minute provisions if you are out for a full day or overnight, moreover, on your way here be sure not to miss the Top 'O' The Rest for hot rolls and excellent coffee.

The route

The eastern shore as far as Stuckbeg (a small beach with an off-grid house) is a pleasant paddle with easy access to and from the water for stops. Beyond Stuckbeg is 5km of inaccessible waterway, shielded by steep-sided banks and regularly vertical rock faces. Before undertaking this section it is important to be aware of prevailing wind and weather conditions. As you round the corner at Rubha na Beithe the relative shelter of Loch Goil can give way to funnelling winds from further down the system.

The west side of the loch is more commonly paddled, with regularly changing scenery and views of the mountains that lie to the west. Toward the mouth of the loch is Carrick, holiday village and home of historic ruins of Carrick Castle. For those on a day trip, Carrick can be an ideal lunch spot with public toilets and easy access. Cormonachan Point often plays home to the resident seals basking on the rocks at low tide.

Be sure to give ample berth to Douglas Pier as you come back toward the head of the loch, as this is a military establishment.

The direction of travel should depend largely on the prevailing wind. Crossing this loch is possible at a number of locations, but it can be deceptively wide and has regular powered craft moving around, so care should be taken.

 River Eachaig | Gill Barrow

28 River Eachaig

Get on / off	NS 142 871 / NS 142 849 or NS 153 830
Time required	3+ hours
Distance	3.5km or 6.5km
Parking / shuttle	NS 142 871 / NS 143 848 or NS 153 830
Grade	1–2

Introduction

This short meandering river is often overlooked by paddlers but is well worth the visit. The river used to be a major route linking the Holy Loch and the Clyde with the Royal Burgh of Inveraray. The route was even used by Mary Queen of Scots in 1563.

About 1.5km down the river is Benmore House. The botanical gardens here are a tourist attraction and this would be a good place for a lunch break and a wander.

As the river flows into the Holy Loch it passes under the A815 at Cot House. Before the bridge was here a ferryman would punt passengers across the river. The Cot House Inn, the pub here, would have been the house of the ferryman so he was always on hand.

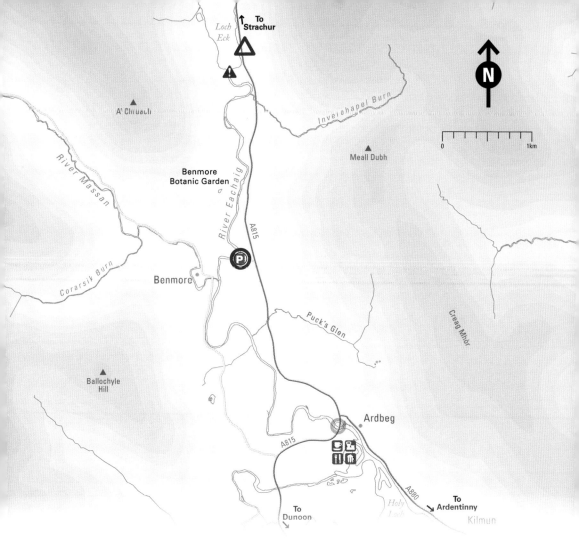

Trip overview

Access from the A815 at the south-eastern point of Loch Eck and paddle across the loch to a small man-made weir, easily portaged river right. (Portage recommended!)

The River Eachaig flows out of Loch Eck, through the Benmore Botanic Gardens and down to meet the sea at the Holy Loch. This gentle white water is often used as an introduction to river paddling, or as part of a longer journey. The river is formed of meandering blind bends with shallow rocky rapids.

The route

Once you've passed the weir, head downstream past the Stratheck Holiday Park on your left. The river deepens beyond here and builds speed through some fast chutes and some blind bends. Be careful as some of these bends can push towards overgrown bushes.

Before long you reach a slower section through the botanic gardens, by Benmore House. Egress is possible here, but it's usually preferable to continue to Uig Hall (NS 142 849) just past the main rapid of the river, a broken weir (grade 2).

This weir is often runnable on the left, but inspection and portage is possible on both sides, although river right is usually easier. This is a great training spot, with a good size pool after it and only a short stint to the get-out.

Below Uig Hall the river flattens out and meanders down to the Holy Loch past the Cot House Caravan Park and pub. You can either egress here up a steep bank, or paddle onto the loch and get out at either Kilmun or Sandbank.

📷 *Kiss from a rose, Loch Goil \ Photo Matt Kilpatrick*

© Portage Falls of Dochart \ Photo PaddleMore

Expedition Routes

These multi-day routes combine elements of three or more other trips from throughout the book. While many of the routes detailed already can be turned easily into an overnight, these six routes have been specially selected as encompassing particularly interesting areas of the national park. They are either especially beautiful, particularly interesting, or just really good paddling. Or, most likely, they're all three.

We have left an element of the planning up to you as the paddler, but there is a section on expeditioning back in the introduction which we recommend you read before heading out, especially if you have limited expeditioning experience. These trips are lengthy and include challenging, tiring sections of paddling as well as some long portages. We strongly recommend that these are undertaken by or along with experienced paddlers who are willing to take responsibility for the group. While we have recommended camping spots, we have also left the length of the trip fairly open. These trips can be taken at a reasonable pace, but also if you are the sort of person who loves a long and physically demanding day, they can be done much quicker. If in doubt, err on the side of caution and plan for shorter days. There are often many options for camping and your route should remain flexible.

As well as camping, some of these routes have the option of staying in accommodation, either bunkhouses or hotels. Where these exist, we have noted them. Similarly with shops, pubs and cafés, you should note where these are and plan to have enough food with you, so that if they are closed when you reach them you don't go hungry.

We have described the routes even where previous pages describe the loch or river, but they are sometimes less detailed than their original entry. We recommend going back and reading the more detailed pages on these routes, and have directed you to the relevant pages.

Expedition paddling is one of the most enjoyable ways to journey around the national park, and takes you back to the essence of why people first paddled. You will have some amazing moments and some serious challenges, but enjoy every minute of it; we wish we were there with you.

The trips

A Viking Loop

B Trossachs Traverse

C Trossachs Loop

D Rob Roy Explore

E Cowal Circuit

F National Park West to East

Sunrise on Loch Venacher \ Photo PaddleMore

Winter on Loch Lomond \ Photo PaddleMore

A Viking Loop

Get on / off	NN 321 045
Time required	4–5 days
Distance	85km
Parking / shuttle	NN 321 045

Introduction

Perhaps the last thing the island dwellers on Loch Lomond expected was to see a fleet of Viking ships sailing down the loch to pillage their homes, but one day the bearded warriors appeared on their shores. How did they get there, and why?

Realising the potential wealth and lack of defences around Loch Lomond, the Vikings raided Arrochar, at the head of Loch Long, before portaging over to Tarbet. The name Tarbet itself comes from Gaelic for isthmus, or, if you want the long form, 'small strip of land connecting two larger bodies of land separated by water'. From here, to the surprise of the inhabitants, they spent three days raiding, looting and killing their way down the

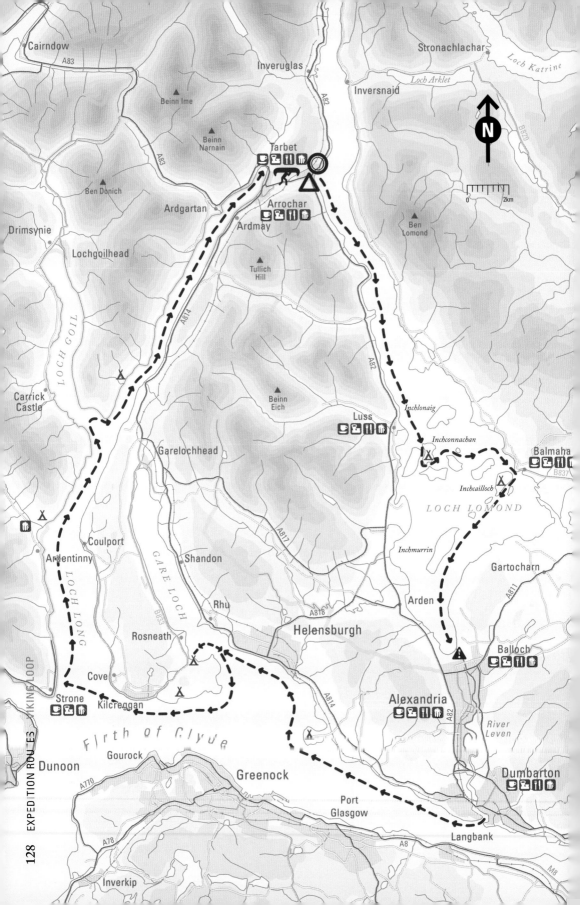

VIKING LOOP

Cairndow
A83
Stronachlachar
Loch Katrine
Inveruglas
Inversnaid
Loch Arklet
Beinn Ime
Beinn Narnain
Ben Donich
Tarbet
A83
Ardgartan
A814
Arrochar
Ardmay
Drimsynie
Lochgoilhead
Ben Lomond
Tullich Hill
LOCH GOIL
Beinn Eich
Carrick Castle
Inchlonaig
Luss
Garelochhead
Inchconnachan
Balmaha
B837
Inchcailloch
LOCH LOMOND
Coulport
A817
Ardentinny
Shandon
Inchmurrin
Gartocharn
Arden
A811
GARE LOCH
LOCH LONG
Rhu
A818
Balloch
Strone
Cove
Kilcreggan
Rosneath
B833
A814
Helensburgh
Alexandria
A82
River Leven
Firth of Clyde
Dumbarton
Gourock
A770
Greenock
A814
Port Glasgow
Langbank
A78
Inverkip
A8
M8

N

0   2km

loch, before escaping down the River Leven.

On their escape, outside of the now National Park boundary, a vicious wind blew them into Largs, where they were set upon by Scottish troops and a bloody battle ensued. Perhaps this, or maybe the fact that the Viking stronghold on Europe was coming to an end, meant this was the final Viking raid on Scotland.

Although we paddle this with very different intentions, it is interesting to explore a similar route, taking in many of the islands across the geological boundary on Loch Lomond, and heading down the river to the Firth of Clyde, which connects Glasgow to the sea.

Trip overview

Being a circular route, this trip can be started at any point. We have selected Tarbet as a logical point with ample parking, access and facilities on hand. Luss, Milarrochy Bay, Dumbarton or anywhere on Loch Long would also suffice.

The Clyde and the lower reaches of Loch Long can be quite unpredictable, but otherwise this trip is inland. Your choice of route on Loch Lomond may be influenced by the weather.

The route

Head off from Tarbet and follow the western shore in a southerly direction. About halfway to Firkin Point you pass Rob Roy's Prison, on the opposite, eastern shore, where he kept the substitute-sheriff of Dumbartonshire prisoner for a week. Continue south past Firkin Point and the Inverbeg holiday park, which sits on a spit of land out from the village. Opposite Inverbeg is Roardennan, which has a hotel and toilets available.

Continue south all the way to Luss and set off across the island chain. There are so many interesting facts to say about all of these islands, and we strongly recommend reading the Beautiful South and Island Explore routes to get a full and colourful history of this part of the loch. Once you reach Balmaha, head back across Inchcailloch, Torrinch, Creinch and Inchmurrin, before heading south toward Balloch and the start of the Leven.

Of course, you can keep following the western shore from Luss. It's a slightly more direct route, but to get a full Viking feeling, we feel it's important to visit some islands.

Follow the route of the Leven down to Dumbarton, then beyond to the Firth of Clyde. As you pass through Balloch, at the start of the river, there is a barrage which needs to be portaged (river right). The river is a gentle meander with a few faster flowing sections of water and is covered in more detail on page (46).

While the Firth of Clyde is far enough inland that the tides are not like those of the sea, they still generate enough power to turn a gentle paddle into an exhausting slog. We recommend checking tide times and aiming to paddle this section at either slack tide or on a retreating current (or to phrase it in nautical parlance, an ebbing tide).

Once onto the Firth of Clyde, turn right along the northern shore and paddle along to Cardross, just prior to the crossing of mouth of Gareloch, or Kilcreggan just after it; both have potential camping. Kilcreggan has an actual campsite and fantastic chip shop. (Gareloch is the home of Faslane, the military submarine base).

The crossing, when you reach Loch Long, is roughly 2km. This is no small undertaking and the traffic and potential weather conditions mean this can require serious thought. It is a necessary crossing, however, as paddling close to Coulport is forbidden, a rule enforced by police and military vessels; they have guns and we recommend listening to them.

Once over to the west of the loch, follow the shoreline north. Camping can be either at Shepherd's Point by Ardentinny, or Mark's Cottage, both covered in previous chapters.

Once you arrive at Arrochar you have the final portage up and over the hill to return to Tarbet. The canny among you may realise at this point that it is far easier to collect the vehicle from Tarbet, load the boats in Arrochar and enjoy a well earned drink in one of the many cafés or pubs available. Obviously this is possible only if you have chosen to start and finish your trip here.

For more in depth information see:

Loch Lomond

River Leven

Loch Long

A sunny day on Loch Lomond | Photo PaddleMore

B Trossachs Traverse

Get on / off	NS 386 822 / NN 668 044
Time required	2–4 days
Distance	80km
Parking / shuttle	NS 385 824 / NN 668 045

Introduction

Not only is this one of the best expeditions within the National Park it is also one of Scotland's classics. The 80km trip starts on the world-famous Loch Lomond, undoubtedly the centrepiece of the park, before crossing four other lochs and down two rivers. The portage from Loch Lomond to Loch Arklet is a challenging uphill route, but you will be rewarded with some classic Trossachs paddling.

Once you cross to Loch Katrine you follow the network which used to take drinking water to Glasgow, and end up on the River Teith, passing through the tourist town of Callander.

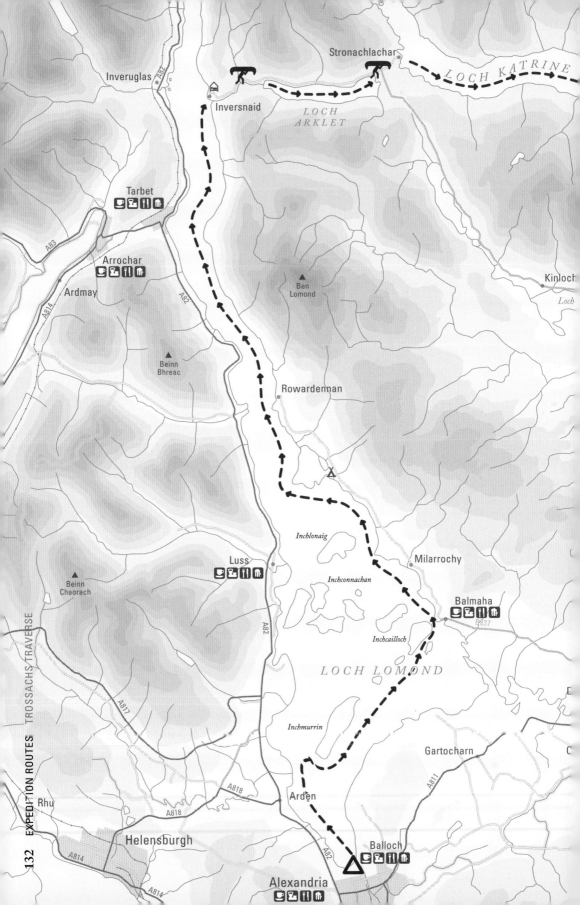

Inveruglas

Inversnaid

Stronachlachar

LOCH KATRINE

LOCH ARKLET

Tarbet

Arrochar

Ardmay

A83

A82

Ben Lomond

Kinloch

Loch

Beinn Bhreac

Rowardennan

Beinn Chaorach

Inchlonaig

Inchconnachan

Milarrochy

Luss

Inchcailloch

Balmaha

B837

LOCH LOMOND

A817

Inchmurrin

Gartocharn

A811

A818

Arden

Rhu

A818

A814

Helensburgh

A82

Balloch

Alexandria

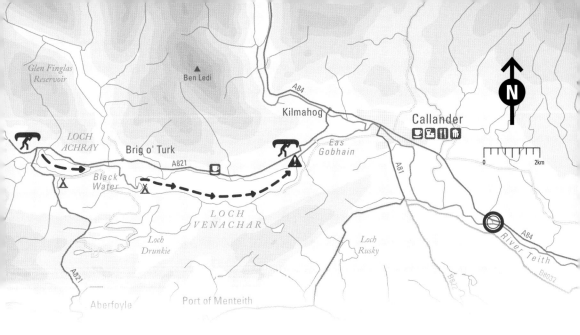

This is a real mixed bag of a trip, some of the lochs are huge and open, while others will feel very secluded and as though you're on your own private pond. The two rivers differ massively, from the woodland adventure of the Black Water to the friendly white water you encounter on the Teith.

Trip overview

Launching in Balloch at the Duncan Mills Memorial Slipway where there is ample secure parking, you can make your way along the first of five lochs before heading up to the highest loch in the Trossachs and then linking the lochs with up to four rivers before arriving either in Callander or Doune.

Taking between two and four days, there are opportunities for wild camping or accommodation for the traveller seeking comfort. Don't underestimate the two portages.

The route

Starting from Balloch, there are a number of options to cover the almost 30km to Inversnaid. The most direct is also one of the more wind affected. Head up the western shore to Auchentullich before crossing to Inchmurrin, site of the Haggis Hurling world record. Follow the chain of small islands up to Inchcailloch and across to Balmaha. From Balmaha, follow the eastern shores up to Milarrochy then Sallochy, a great camping option for those who want to split this section of the trip into two parts.

Leaving Sallochy, you still have 16km to cover to get to Inversnaid. The road ends at Rowadennan and you are slightly more exposed from here. However, the Rob Roy way continues to follow the shoreline and there are plenty of opportunities to stop and take refuge from incoming weather if necessary.

From Inversnaid Hotel it's time to give the arms a rest and get those legs moving on the 2.5km long portage with 175m of ascent to Loch Arklet. Roughly halfway on this portage is Inversnaid, a small village complete with bunkhouse. This can offer accommodation, or alternatively a coffee or breakfast stop along the way.

The best thing about reaching Loch Arklet is that it marks the high point of this trip. and the short paddle along the loch is a great rest for the legs before making the fairly straightforward 1.5km portage downhill to Loch Katrine.

Head south-east towards the foot of Loch Katrine from where you can either start walking again or follow the Achray Water (Grd2/3) down onto Loch Achray. It does need to have been raining quite heavily in order to paddle the Achray Water and it can be quite a technical section, so be prepared to spend some time on the banks scouting and lining down this section.

Loch Achray spills out into the Black Water. The gentle flow and shingley rapids will carry you comfortably downstream, but watch out for overhanging branches and fallen trees, especially around blind bends. The river meanders and loses most of its power as you join Loch Venachar, the final loch of this epic journey. At the eastern end of the loch you will need to portage the waterworks in order to join the Eas Gobhain.

The Eas Gobhain flows under a bridge and there is immediately a grade 2 rock shelf rapid. This is the most technical section of the river, but the whole thing is renowned for being shallow and often overgrown with trees. Be prepared to get out of your boat and use ropes to get downriver. After consistent heavy rain this can become a difficult place to paddle, with limited opportunities to stop and loads of trees and branches in the water.

Eas Gobhain joins the River Teith at the Meadows. You can either finish your trip here in Callander, with a pie and coffee from Mhor Bread, or if you have fuel left in the tank follow the Teith down to either egress point.

For more in depth information see:

Loch Lomond

Loch Arklet

Loch Katrine

Loch Achray

Blackwater

Loch Venachar

River Teith

C Trossachs Loop

Get on / off	NN 598 061
Time required	3–4 days
Distance	65km
Parking / shuttle	NN 598 061

Introduction

This circumnavigation of the Trossachs will test your paddling skills as well as your grit and determination. It includes open water, rivers both up and downstream, and a serious portage.

The Victorian waterworks which once carried water from Loch Katrine to Glasgow now makes up the first half of this trip, albeit in reverse. After a quick visit to Rob Roy's birth place at the head of the Loch Katrine, this route portages up and over the hills to Loch Doine, where he lived out the end of his life, before flowing down through Balquhidder, his final resting place. The final stretch follows the Rob Roy way southwards down toward Callander, the historic highland boundary town.

Trip overview

This circuit starts on Loch Venachar and heads round to join up with the Rob Roy Explore expedition route. Follow the Rob Roy Explore completely, finishing on the River Teith (this requires a shuttle) or, if you want to close the loop, you will need to head upstream on the Eas Gobhain. This is a shallow, overgrown river with a grade 2 ledge at the top, and will test your upstream skills and determination after a multi-day trip. As the Leny joins the River Teith at Callander, turn right and head up the other fork which joins at the same time; this is the Eas Gobhain.

An alternative to avoid shuttling or any upstream antics would be to finish the Leny at Kilmahog (see page 98) and follow the Rob Roy way back toward Loch Venachar to collect your vehicle.

The trip could be completed in either direction, both involve upstream travel, but by going clockwise we limit this to more manageable rivers and allow ourselves to paddle the really fun ones.

The route

Set off across Loch Venachar sticking to the southern shores. Watch out for other water users as you pass the sailing club and the scout centre. After six kilometres of open water you come to the bottom of the Black Water. This is almost as hard to find as is the top on Loch Achray.

Once you find the outflow of the river, start the upstream battle. Most of the river is paddleable, especially after a decent rainfall, but fallen trees often need portaging and some shallower or more powerful rapids may require walking around or lining your boat up.

It's a wonderful sense of relief when you reach Loch Achray and the gentle open water, but it's just a short stint here before you have to climb out of your boat and begin the portage.

From the Ben Venue car park (NN 506 068) there is a platformed trail which may not be the most direct route, but avoids much of the narrow and blind road up to Loch Katrine. It would also be suitable for a trolley. Regardless, some of this portage is on the road, so be extremely careful, especially during the busier summer months.

Access Loch Katrine at the south east end and paddle out through the narrows, avoiding any conflict with the *Sir Walter Scott* (or Queen Victoria!).

Loch Katrine is the longest body of water on this trip and the waves can become quite large in windy conditions. Stick to the northern shore and make use of the bays to afford yourself some shelter, following the almost ten kilometres until you are level with the Black Island.

Drag or carry your boat up the Allt a Choin to the small lochan at the top of the hill. Head down the other side to the top of the River Larig and paddle / line your boat downstream, depending on flow, to Loch Doine, where you join the Rob Roy Explore Route down to Callander via Loch Voil, the Balvaig, Loch Lubnaig and the River Leny.

For more in depth information see:

Loch Venachar

The Blackwater

Loch Achray

Loch Katrine

Loch Doine and Voil,

River Balvaig

Loch Lubnaig

River Leny

River Teith

D Rob Roy Explore

Get on / off	NN 443 182 / NN 668 044
Time required	2–3 days
Distance	40km
Parking / shuttle	NN 445 184 / NN 668 045

Introduction

Travel through true Rob Roy Territory! Starting from the site of his house at Inverlochlarig, set off down Loch Doine and Voile, past his burial place in Balquhidder, the village in which he lived out the last of his days. The Rob Roy Way, a long distance walking route, follows almost all of this multi day paddling trip, and there are plenty of opportunities to hop off and explore on foot.

Rob Roy has cropped up a great deal throughout the book, and not without reason. He lived out most of his life right here in the Trossachs, and many of his escapades took place within the national park.

This area is renowned too for wildlife, with red squirrel, deer and many birds of prey, including the occasional osprey.

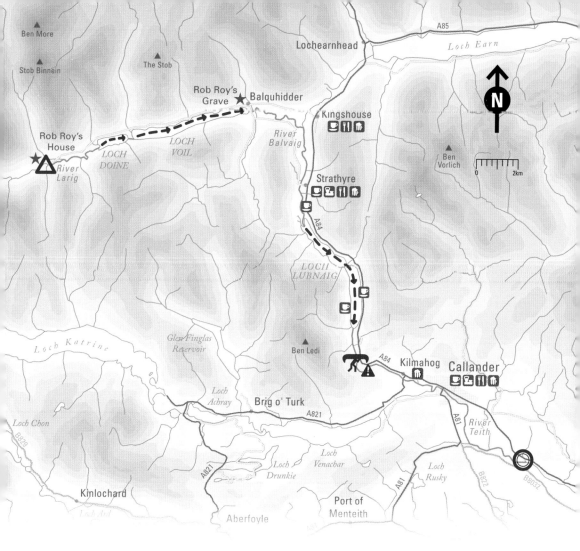

Trip overview

A fairly relaxed trip, mostly. The trip starts in the seclusion of Loch Doine before spending much of the journey following the course of the A84. This is one of the shorter expeditions in this section, and can be made into a relatively straightforward two-day trip by getting out at the end of Loch Lubnaig.

The sections after this, of the Leny and the Teith, are more challenging sections, and the Leny especially may warrant portaging. The trip finishes beyond Callander at the Teith egress, or you can continue down to Deanston.

The route

Leave Inverlochlarig and set off down the gentle stretch of river which flows 2km into Loch Doine. Once you emerge out into Loch Doine, pick a shore to follow eastwards and into the narrows which connects you to Loch Voile. Enjoy the seclusion of these two narrow lochs, and be sure to hop out at the old church in Balquhidder and visit the grave of Rob Roy before you enter the Balvaig (grade 1).

This mellow river hides you with steep banks and you feel as though you're in the middle of nowhere as you meander through its many bends. The usual egress point for the Balvaig is next to the Broch café, perfect for dinner, before finding somewhere to camp. Also on the river is the village of Strathyre, with pubs, hotels and a small local shop.

Head out onto Loch Lubnaig and follow the west shore all the way south. As you pass the narrows the loch bends noticeably and you will be able to see the end of it, where a car park and café sit on the eastern shore. This is a perfect finish point for those who don't want to negotiate the white water of the Leny or the Teith.

The River Leny has some serious white water, with a three kilometre section graded 3/4 with a grade 5 falls in the middle. We recommend reading the guide for the Leny (page 98) and if necessary, portage down the Rob Roy Way which follows the course of the river to Kilmahog. From here the river mellows out and flows into the Teith at Callander.

Join the Teith (grade 2) and head downstream under the red stone bridge that signifies the true entrance to the river. The gentle white water and sweepings bends will carry you down to the end of this trip, the egress of the River Teith, where the river reconnects with the road, just before Drumvaich. This is just after the main rapid of the river which either runs river left, or can be portaged over a stone shelf on the right.

For more in depth information see:

Lochs Doine and Voile

River Balvaig

Loch Lubnaig

River Leny

River Teith

Paddlers on Loch Eck | Photo Paddlemore

E Cowal Circuit

Get on / off	NS 141 946 / Lochgoilhead NN 199 013 or Loch Long NN 294 048
Time required	2–3 days
Distance	45km
Parking end	NN 727 014 or NN 294 048

Introduction

One of the many hidden gems of Scottish overnight paddlesports trips exploring one of the routes less paddled, where you're sure to have a true adventure. Starting up at the head of Loch Eck, this trip navigates fresh water, river and sea lochs, finishing inland at Lochgoilhead, or alternatively at Arrochar.

The sea lochs are home to all sorts of wildlife and it's not uncommon to be joined on this trip by seals, porpoise, gulls and terns, among others. Whales have been seen in Loch Long on several occasions, although this is a rarity.

This route is steeped in history, from the Paper Caves on Loch Eck, the hiding place of ancient land entitlements, to the 15th century centre of Christianity that is the Holy Loch.

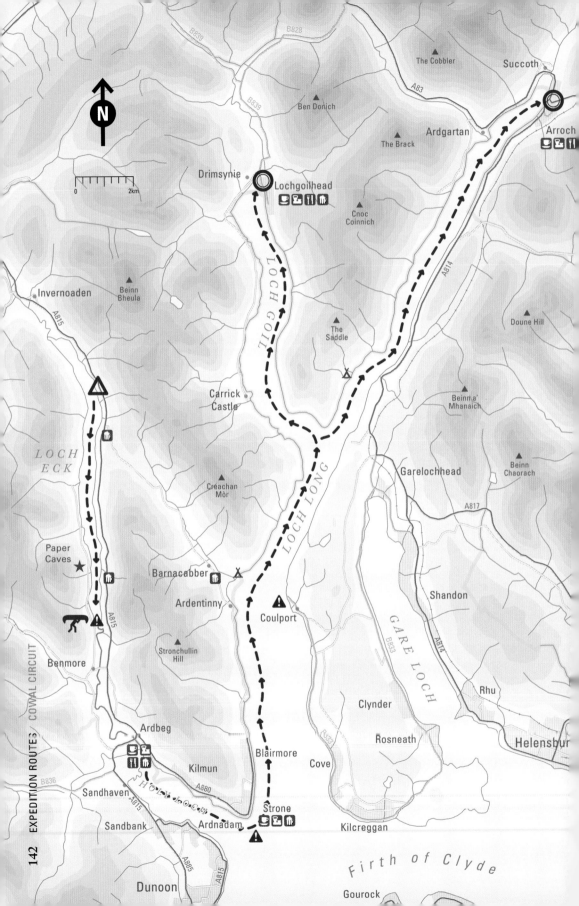

N

0   2km

The Cobbler

Succoth

A83

Ardgartan

Arroch

Ben Donich

B839

B828

The Brack

Drimsynie

Lochgoilhead

Cnoc Coinnich

A814

Doune Hill

Invernoaden

Beinn Bheula

A815

LOCH GOIL

The Saddle

Beinn a' Mhanaich

Beinn Chaorach

Carrick Castle

LOCH ECK

Garelochhead

A817

Paper Caves

Creachan Mòr

LOCH LONG

Shandon

Barnacabber

Ardentinny

Coulport

GARE LOCH

B833

A814

Benmore

A815

Stronchullin Hill

Clynder

Rhu

Ardbeg

Rosneath

Helensbur

Kilmun

Blairmore

Cove

A880

Sandhaven

HOLY LOCH

Strone

Kilcreggan

Sandbank

Ardnadam

A815

A885

B836

Firth of Clyde

Dunoon

Gourock

Out on Loch Long and Loch Goil, a military presence is often noticeable. Submarines make their way here from Faslane, round on Gareloch, for testing and routine maintenance.

These are busy waters and you're rarely short of something to see as you follow the Cowal Circuit.

Trip overview

Incorporating both freshwater and tidal waterways, this expedition exposes you to all that the West Coast of Scotland has to offer. This varied trip takes you from the relative shelter of Loch Eck to the vastness of the Firth of Clyde before heading inland, following the abundant wildlife to finish either in Lochgoilhead, or Arrochar at the head of Loch Long itself.

Conditions can be treacherous, especially on the more exposed elements. The peninsula where the Holy Loch turns onto Loch Long has an enormous fetch and large waves can form with winds coming in off the Firth of Clyde.

The route

Launch at Dornoch Point and paddle south down whichever side of Loch Eck you choose. The west side, notably by the Paper Caves, provides great camping for those setting off late in the day looking to make a few kilometres of headway. This narrow loch can funnel winds so be ready for a battle!

Leaving Loch Eck, portage the weir and join the Eachaig. Once past the broken weir by Uig Hall, this river gently meanders before flowing into the Holy Loch. Follow the northern shore to Strone, where a left turn takes you onto Loch Long.

For those who don't know this section of water, or haven't read the Holy Loch entry, here is our PaddleMore weather warning:

"Be very aware of weather conditions before leaving Gibb's Point, just further along from Graham's Point. Shortly after Gibb's Point, the beach gives way to a high Victorian sea wall and there is no escape point until you round the bend. The wind here comes straight off the Clyde and can push against rocks and the wall here with incredible ferocity."

The prevailing winds should now generally be in your favour and help carry you up to your chosen camp spot. For many this will be Shepherd's Point, Ardentinny. For those who wish to push on further there are two options.

If you are headed up Loch Goil to finish at Lochgoilhead there is camping as you enter the loch and public toilets can be found in Carrick.

For those finishing in Arrochar, Long Long, head past the mouth of Loch Goil and look out for Mark's Cottage on your left after 2km, opposite the piers at Coulport. Here

© Campfire \ Photo Neil McLaren

you will find a bothy and ample camping. This is a popular bothy and commonly used by groups, so be prepared to camp if necessary.

Follow your chosen loch to its culmination, enjoying the views of the surrounding mountains. Both villages have pubs and shops to enjoy a well-earned reward.

For more in depth information see:

Loch Eck,

River Eachaig,

Holy Loch,

Loch Long,

Loch Goil

This was our first canoe expedition together, and

Moose's first ever canoe expedition.

F National Park West to East

Get on / off	NS 113 979 / NN 668 044
Time required	5–6 days
Distance	110km
Parking / shuttle	NS 112 979 / NN 624 079

Introduction

At over one hundred kilometres and including nine lochs, four rivers and three sizable portages, this is no mean feat. Crossing from the western boundary of the park, all the way to Callander in the east takes on some of the largest and most scenic lochs. This also encompasses several sections of other long distance routes along the way.

Trip overview

This trip sets off from the head of Loch Eck, heads up Loch Long, across Loch Lomond and then loops the Trossachs, ending up on the River Teith. The portages cross difficult ground and can be steep in places. You will need a good level of fitness for this trip.

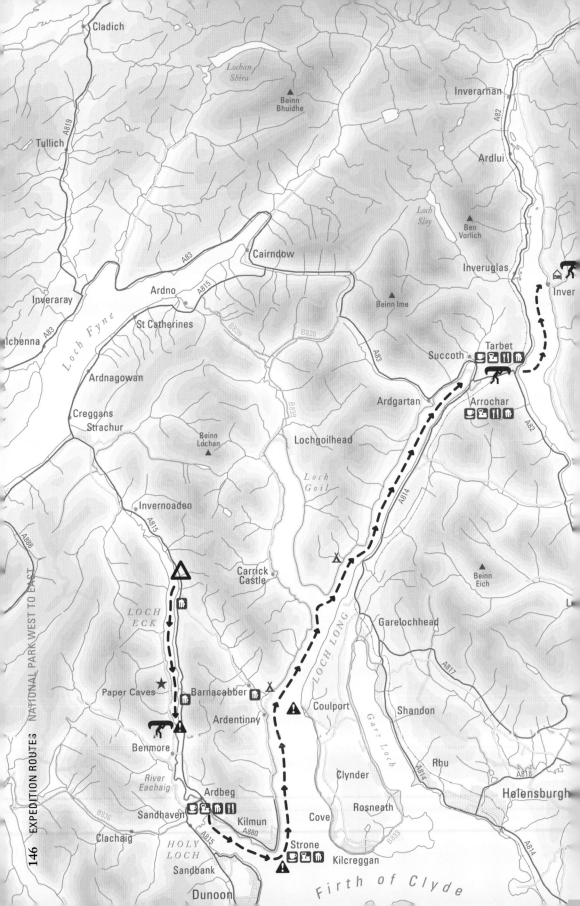

Cladich

Tullich

A819

Inveraray

Ichenna

A83

Loch Fyne

Ardno

Ardnagowan

A815

St Catherines

Creggans
Strachur

Invernoaden

A815

A886

LOCH
ECK

Paper Caves

Barnacabber

Ardentinny

Benmore

River
Eachaig

B836

Ardbeg

Sandhaven

Clachaig

HOLY
LOCH

Sandbank

A815

Dunoon

Kilmun

A880

Strone

Kilcreggan

Cove

Lochan
Shira

Beinn
Bhuidhe

A83

B839

Cairndow

Beinn Ime

B828

B839

Lochgoilhead

Loch
Goil

Carrick
Castle

Coulport

LOCH LONG

A814

Garelochhead

Gare Loch

Clynder

Rosneath

Firth of Clyde

Ardlui

Loch
Sloy

Ben
Vorlich

A82

Inveruglas

Inver

Succoth

Tarbet

Ardgartan

Arrochar

A814

Beinn
Eich

A82

Shandon

Rhu

A814

A817

A818

Helensburgh

Balquhidder

River
Balvaig

Kingshouse

LOCH
DOINE

LOCH
VOIL

River
Larig

nn a'
roin

Ben
Vorlich

Strathyre

A84

LOCH
LUBNAIG

enachiachar

LOCH KATRINE

Glen
Finglas
Reservoir

Ben Ledi

Kilmahog

Callander

CH
KLET

B829

Loch
Chon

Ben
Venue

Loch Venachar

River
Teith

A84

Brig o' Turk

A821

Loch
Drunkie

Port of Menteith

A81

B822

B803

Kinlochard

Aberfoyle

Loch
Ard

Braeval

Lake of
Menteith

Thornhill

B8034

Gartmore

A81

A811

Arnprior

Kippen

Milarrochy

Buchlyvie

B822

Balmaha

B837

Balfron

B818

Fintry

N

Gartocharn

Drymen

Croftamie

Killearn

A811

Dumgoyne

A81

Strathblane

Lennoxtown

andria

0   4km

Being such a big trip we obviously recommend you are thoroughly prepared before you set off. There are plenty of spots to camp along the way, as well as a handful of options if you want to splash some cash and have a slightly more comfortable night. Arrochar, roughly a third of the way through the trip, and Strathyre, toward the end of the route, both have local shops where you can top up supplies, but we recommend setting out with enough stock to keep yourself going. Keep some spares in case you end up windbound at camp; while it's not especially common, it's not unheard of on some of these lochs.

The route

Head south on Loch Eck and wave goodbye to your car for a few days. Follow the western shore all the way until you reach the Eachaig, portaging the weir on river right. Enter this river and navigate its many twists and turns. After the main feature, the broken weir by Uig Hall, the river mellows out and meanders its way down to the Holy Loch.

Passing the sand banks which form by the outflow, follow the north side of the Holy Loch, until you reach the corner where it joins Loch Long. In case you've not read the Holy Loch entry earlier in the book, we'll repeat what we said before.

"Be very aware of weather conditions before leaving Gibb's Point, just further along from Graham's Point. Shortly after Gibb's Point, the beach gives way to a high Victorian sea wall and there is no escape point until you round the bend. The wind here comes straight off the Clyde and can push against rocks and the wall here with incredible ferocity."

Once you turn into Loch Long, you will usually have a decent tailwind to carry along. Follow north past Ardentinny and across the mouth of Loch Goil, then past Mark's Cottage. There are plenty of overnight spots around all three of these places. Keep to the west shore as you pass Coulport.

From Mark's Cottage keep to the western shore and head all the way up to Arrochar. This is the first major portage. It's about three kilometres from Arrochar to Tarbet, and you'll probably want a trolley for this one.

Set off again on Loch Lomond, crossing straight away to Rowchoish and follow the shore north to Inversnaid. This is portage number two. We realise that it's soon after number one, but most people will spend a night on the shores of Loch Lomond before attempting the second portage. Some masochists however, may enjoy a whole day of portaging; it certainly gets it out the way.

The hill up to Loch Arklet is steep and it's a welcome relief to stop for a drink or some food at Inversnaid bunkhouse. If you've smashed out both of the portages in a day, you may wish to reward yourself with a night here in a real bed.

Head across Loch Arklet and cross the short distance to Loch Katrine. Here it's just a couple of kilometres to the Black Island and the start of the final portage. Drag or carry your boat up the Allt a Choin to the small lochan at the top of the hill. Head down the other side to the top of the River Larig and paddle / line your boat downstream, depending on flow, to Loch Doine.

Cross Loch Doine and head down the narrows to Loch Voile, another loch with plenty of available wild camping. Leave down the Balvaig and wind your way down to Loch Lubnaig.

The crooked Loch is probably the last part of the trip we would recommend camping on, once you head into the Leny you're committed to continue to the end of the trail.

The River Leny is serious white water, and you may choose to portage some or most of the river. We recommend reading the guide for the Leny and making your own decision, but the Rob Roy Way follows the river and would be perfect for a trolley route.

The end of the Leny is much more mellow and joins the River Teith in the Meadows above Callander. Stop here for a well-earned pie or a coffee before negotiating the River Teith to the end of this trip.

For more in depth information see:

Loch Eck,

River Eachaig,

Holy Loch,

Loch Long,

Loch Lomond,

Loch Arklet,

Loch Katrine,

Loch Doine and Voile,

River Balvaig,

Loch Lubnaig,

River Leny,

River Teith

© Falls of Falloch \ Photo PaddleMore

The Great Scottish Midge

Your tent is set up; water boils gently on the stove. The sun drops below the hills on the far side of the water, the last rays reflect off the unbroken surface of water and the temperature drops to a pleasant eleven degrees.

Through the dusk, a shadow looms over the water. You know it's too late, you've been spotted. The cloud approaches. You hurry to do what you must. Pasta, almost cooked, is drained and poured into a bowl, the stove extinguished and thrown haphazardly into the tent porch. You take one last look around to make sure everything is in order before you lurch into your tent, zipping it closed behind you as you hear the first tap on your fly sheet. But it's not rain you hear. It's something much more sinister.

You've just escaped the Great Scottish Midge.

The Scottish Highland Midge is the number one predator in the country. They have four rows of savage teeth and five thousand midges could overcome a highland cow and drain it of blood in less than five minutes. The collective noun for a group of midges is an "Oh No". The largest midge ever recorded was roughly the size of a five pence piece and the most bites ever recorded on a human being was impossible to count since no one can stand still for that long once they've been bitten.

None of those things are true, or probably not. The bit about not being able to stand still is fairly apt. However, if you've come into contact with a bite of midges (the correct collective noun, suitably), you would probably believe some of them.

In fact, midges are an incredibly important part of the Scottish Highland ecosystem, providing enormous amounts of prey for small birds, bats and larger insects. What's more, most of them don't even bite. The only midges who bite are females on their second, third or fourth cycle of egg laying. Cycle one requires no feeding, but successive egg laying requires a blood meal. The female will land and bite through the skin before injecting an anti-coagulate to prevent the blood from clotting. If left un-swatted, the female will feed for up to five minutes before leaving.

This may all sound relatively normal for an insect, but when these miniscule black dots, roughly a millimetre long, approach you in the thousands you can be sure to feel every single bite. Each individual responds differently to the bite, and we don't just mean whether they wave their arms around and shout and swear a bit. Your body releases histamine to the area, which causes swelling and irritation, the extent of which varies from person to person.

There are hundreds of different midge-preventatives on the market, ranging from smoke-emitting coils and citronella candles, to sprays and creams, to nets and fabrics. All of these do work, sometimes … but the Scottish Midge is a hardy creature, used to challenging environments, and some brave wee souls will fight through the deterrent and do their best to gain a meal.

Fortunately, around water we are often saved by the one thing they can't quite fight against; wind. Midge are small, lightweight and slow moving. Even relatively gentle breeze is enough to see them drop down and hide in the bushes or bracken until conditions calm down. It doesn't need to be blowing a gale, just a few kilometres per hour is enough.

There are midge forecasts and any number of options for you to try to fend off these wee blighters, but many of us who venture out into the highlands of Scotland have long accepted that they are all just part of the fun. After all, nowhere can be perfect, and if the only imperfection we have to deal with is small insects (and very occasionally the odd rain shower), Scotland is still a pretty idealistic place.

Keeping the midge at bay

Midge Nets – If the midge can't get to your skin, it can't bite you, it's that simple. Even if you're using other means of repelling the midge, these nets stop them from buzzing around your ears, nose and eyes which can sometimes be more irritating than the actual biting.

Long Clothing – Along the same lines as the head nets, long sleeves and trousers stop the midge from getting to your skin. Tucking your trousers into your socks can help too.

DEET Spray Repellents – There are a number of different spray options which repel insects, most of which contain some form of DEET. These are effective at stopping you being bitten, but the effects of DEET on your skin can be worse than the effects of the bites. Long-term use can also eat away at kit and clothing.

Smidge Spray – Smidge is one of the most popular forms of repellent for midge. It works by blocking receptors of biting insects to throw them off your scent.

Citronella – Citronella candles repel insects in a limited area, while natural sprays can stop them biting you. These sprays usually have to be applied more frequently than synthetic alternatives.

Smoke – Smoke from specially-made coils can deter all insects, as can smoke from fires. The downside is that you tend to have to be in the line of the smoke or very close to the fire for this to have effect. Remember, if you plan to have a fire, make sure they are permitted where you are camping and follow Leave No Trace principles.

Wind – Short of carrying a fan with you, it's hard to artificially cause this, but camping in open and breezy areas, rather than the usual sheltered and enclosed spots we search for, might make your evening more comfortable. This choice is weather dependent, of course. There's sometimes more pressing matters than a few midges when it comes to choosing a campsite!

Camping Management Zone

Scotland's Land Reform Act is seen as being some of the most forward thinking access legislation in the world. It allows those who are using the land for a recreational purpose (this includes commercial users leading recreational sport or activities) to freely and responsibly access the hills, lochs and rivers of Scotland, using non-motorised means of travel (exceptions are made for powered wheel-chairs, etc). Unfortunately, as we know, not everyone in society shares the same meaning for being responsible which led to the National Park Authority confronted with a large number of issues including antisocial behaviour, and damage being caused within the Park by a small sector of the Park users.

In 2017 The National Park Authority was granted permission by the Scottish Government to enact the Camping Management Byelaw which covers four percent of the landmass of the Park. This land mass tends to be the area around the loch, between the loch shores and major roads, where it is far too easy for people to stop their car, unload their large tent and metric tonne of Buckfast Tonic Wine and try to start a fire using standing trees.

This irresponsible attitude has lead to the Park introducing the four Camping Management Zones, meaning that between 1 March and 30 September camping within these zones should only happen at designated campsites or within permit zones.

The National Park, as part of the conditions of the byelaw, have made an additional 300 low-cost camping spaces available in addition to the pre-existing commercial sites throughout the Park. Within the permit zones wild camping is available with a permit which can be obtained via the National Parks Website.

The Camping Management Zones are clearly signed throughout the park; however the best thing to do when planning your trip is to check the National Parks Website, and ensure that if you're planning to stay within a Camping Management Zone when on a trip you are doing so correctly, as refusal to comply with the byelaws could result in a report to the Procurator Fiscal and a fine of up to £500.

Gàidhlig

Gàidhlig (Scottish Gaelic) is one of the many ancient languages that has been spoken in Scotland across the centuries. It was the main language spoken in Scotland from around the year 900 until Scots started to creep in around the 14th century. English has been the official language of Scotland since the Act of the Union in 1707.

The west of Scotland, and in particular the islands, still today have native Gàidhlig speakers. You'll still see Gaelic throughout Scotland, mainly on road signs and public service buildings and vehicles, as the Scottish Government is trying hard to keep the language alive, but don't expect to have many conversations in Gaelic as most people in Scotland today know very little if any.

Despite efforts from many over the years to Anglicise the names, many lochs, rivers and hills still have Gaelic in their names. We've therefore created a quick guide to help you understand the landscape and its Gàidhlig names.

Gàidhlig	Translation
Allt	Burn, stream
Abhainn	River
Bealach	pass, route
Beinn	mountain
Beag, bheag	Small
Cnoc	hill
Coire	corrie
Creag	crag, rock
Druim	ridge
Eas	Waterfall
Garbh	Rough
Gleann	Glen, valley (steep)
Mar, mara	Sea
Maol	bare hill, mountain
Meall	lump-shaped hill, mountain
Mòr, Mhòr	Big / large
Slàinte	Cheers!
Sìthean, sìdhean	knoll (often associated with the sìthichean or fairies)
Srath	Strath, valley (wide)
Sruth	Stream
Stob	peak, summit, something sticking up like a post
Tom	hillock
Uisge	Water

Index